ROLLER COASTER HILL

The Road from Rejection to Redemption

Dwaine Casmey

Denver, CO .

Dwaine Casmey, www.rollercoasterhill.com

Editing by Cara Highsmith, Highsmith Creative Services, www.highsmithcreative.com
Cover and Interior Design by Mitchell Shea, atdawndesigns.com

I have tried to recreate events, locales and conversations from my memories of them. In order to maintain their anonymity in some instances I have changed the names of individuals and places, I may have changed some identifying characteristics and details such as physical properties, occupations and places of residence.

Although the author and publisher have made every effort to ensure that the information in this book was correct at press time, the author and publisher do not assume and hereby disclaim any liability to any party for any loss, damage, or disruption caused by errors or omissions, whether such errors or omissions result from negligence, accident, or any other cause.

This book is not intended as a substitute for the medical advice of physicians. The reader should regularly consult a physician in matters relating to his/her health and particularly with respect to any symptoms that may require diagnosis or medical attention.

Printed in the United States of America

ISBN 978-0-692-47051-0

Library of Congress Control Number: 2015910070

First Edition 14 13 12 11 10 / 10 9 8 7 6 5 4 3 2 1

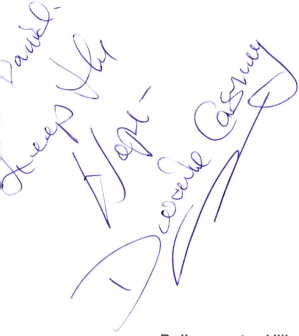

Rollercoaster Hill

Foreword

When Dwaine told me he was writing a book about his story of childhood to present I knew it would be a ride. And of course the title is Rollercoaster Hill.

I met Dwaine in the late 80s soon after his release from prison. At the time I was starting a church in Everett, Washington, and I had a counseling practice that primarily worked with addictions of all types—drugs, alcohol, sex, codependency, you name it. Dwaine was a natural for what I had to offer since he qualified for all of these and more. I first saw Dwaine as a client and as a congregant. We met often working on core issues. My training was in family systems, addressing questions such as, What were the family of origin's systemic patterns? Addiction is most often connected to a deep self-hatred, creating a powerful toxic shame. Dwaine was a classic result of shame-based parenting and what it can produce.

I know that his desire in telling his story is to help others who continue to struggle with self-destructive behaviors. When we tell our stories the intent is not to blame our parents and others, nor is it to minimize our own choices that may have hurt ourselves and others. We simply need to tell the truth. Our addictions hide in and are empowered by our shame. The only way to break its power and find freedom is to tell the whole truth.

I love the stories of people and their journeys from shame to freedom. I have my own story that brought me to be passionate about others finding health and freedom. I know that Dwaine has found freedom through listening to his own story.

Now he wants to share what he has discovered, hoping the reader will find the courage to look at their own lives and hear the voice of God speaking to them, saying: "You are fearfully and wonderfully made."

Dwaine and I do not now live in the same city, he is not a member of my church, and he is no longer a client. Now Dwaine Casmey is my friend and I am proud to know him.

Rich Swetman

Acknowledgements

Thank you to the following: Jim Henderson who believed I had a story to tell.

Cara Highsmith, my very talented editor, who encouraged me to share more than facts by reliving the moments and the feelings I was running from for so long.

Kathy Forbes, my loving and dedicated wife, who comforted me and gave me strength to continue writing this book, especially when my damp eyes kept me from seeing the words on the page.

Those who reached out to me during my journey, some with great risk, and showed me a different kind of love – a love that made all the difference. You know who you are.

Contents

Introduction
MIDNIGHT IN SALEM

It was midnight in Salem, Oregon. I was twenty-one years old. Concealed in my overcoat was a billy club as long as my arm, and I intended to put it to use. I needed money to pay for my hotel. I'd spent my last ten dollars from a home invasion three days earlier on a couple hits of LSD. My plan was to catch someone out late (and hopefully drunk). I'd ask for directions, hit them as hard as I could with the club, and take their cash. I was on autopilot, and in my deranged state, I planned to repeat this behavior until I'd stolen enough money to pay for my hotel. I was exhausted. I desperately needed to sleep. Tomorrow would take care of itself.

There was no warning. The surprise attack went down . . . only, I was the one taken off guard. I was entranced by the image of a small boy standing in his pajamas on the front porch of a big white house. The house faced east and the morning sun lit up the porch and the boy. I was overcome by his innocence. Not a worry, not a care in the world. I looked closely and saw myself in his face. I wondered how that little kid became this guy with a club in his coat. My determination caved, and I sobbed.

Now in my mid-fifties with a successful IT career, I still remember that twenty-one-year-old guy with the club in his coat, starving, tired, and desperate. I'm overwhelmed not only by his lack of values but his profound lack of *personal value.* What happened between that midnight moment in Salem and what I've become today? *What went right?*

This is not a story of a tough guy gone straight. This is the story of what Jesus called "the abundant life" and how I got lucky enough to run into it.

Chapter 1
LEAVING HOME

I left home at the age of sixteen in April 1976. I was just a month or so shy of finishing my junior year in high school. Both of my older brothers were gone and, as I look back, I think my parents were just done raising kids. If they knew even a fraction of the things I was doing behind their backs, the trip to Children's Services Division (CSD) in Dallas, Oregon on that Tuesday morning would have happened much sooner. Getting caught stealing a few dollars from the purse of an old lady cook at a restaurant where I worked gave them the out they were looking for.

On Sunday evening my mom and dad called me into the living room and shared the phone conversation they'd had with the frustrated restaurant manager. As was typically the case, I stood while they sat in their chairs as they expressed their anger and disappointment. I got dizzy from standing so long in one place. (I think they knew it and it was another way of torturing me.) Finally we went into my bedroom where my father started rifling through my dresser drawers searching for whatever he could find to substantiate a decision that most likely was already made.

It didn't take long to uncover a pack of Marlboro cigarettes. Without thinking, I said "Shit!" That resulted in the palm of his hand on the side of my head, which knocked me down to the floor. This was not the first time he hit me and knocked me down, and somehow the blow had lost its sting.

I went to school the next day with the understanding that they would be making a decision about whether or not I would continue living at home. When I returned after school I was handed an empty cardboard box. "Pack your things, Dwaine, tomorrow you're leaving."

You'd think I would be devastated. After all I was getting kicked out of my home just as my oldest brother had shortly after he turned fifteen. Dennis had been caught stealing cigarettes and a bottle of wine from a grocery store. Mom drove him down to Albany, Oregon CSD and handed him over to a juvenile caseworker. I was not given the opportunity to say goodbye. Suddenly, Dennis was just gone.

My next oldest and the middle brother, Danny, survived the madness, graduated from high school in

1975 and landed in the Marine Corp boot camp just days after his graduation ceremony. Danny learned at an early age that it was better just to go with it and not to make waves until you could leave and never look back.

And now it was my turn. It's safe to say that by most people's standards I had not acted out severely enough to warrant being cast out of my home at age sixteen, at least in comparison to others I would encounter in the system in the next twenty months. But I was not innocent by any stretch. I smoked tobacco and pot. I had not yet been drunk, although I had drunk some wine at my aunt's wedding and had a beer at a party. I stole whatever cash was left out in the open and even a watch or two at the dime store. I skipped class incessantly. I never wanted to be home. I wanted freedom from all authority, but mostly that of my parents.

It was the 70s and I was heavily influenced by songs about freedom, sex, drugs, and rock and roll. The songs of Bread, America, Neil Young, and the Eagles called to me from the time I hit preadolescence. In my state of self-indulgence and total lack of self-worth, this music helped me escape from a world that I saw as both angry and frightening, and I found refuge in the melancholy sounds of the 70s mixed with some good Columbian weed.

Many years later my parents made the observation that they believed they might have been able to make a difference if they had put some significant effort into my life, whatever that meant. But they chose not to and didn't say why.

As I prepared to leave my home, I didn't know exactly what my future held, but at least I didn't have to hide my cigarettes anymore. As we drove the short ten miles to Dallas, Oregon that Tuesday morning, there were no thoughts about whether my parents put in enough effort. Nothing like "how can a mother kick a child out of their home?" Nope. My only thought was: *I can smoke without getting into trouble.*

We met the caseworker who would be responsible for me for the next nine months. Roger Mattson listened while my parents used words such as "incorrigible" and "delinquent." He threw back words such as "family counseling" and "therapy." Dad responded with the very definitive words "no" and "He's never coming home, ever." Papers were signed. Hands were shook. Dad's resolve won out without much of a fight; Roger never had a chance. I walked out to the parking lot to get my box of things from the trunk of the car. I can't remember if I hugged my mother, but I know there was no touching my dad.

The last time I hugged him was when I was about six years old. I had held my arms up toward the giant man before he went to work as I had done many times before. He suddenly looked very uncomfortable. He hesitated, embarrassed, and gave me a quick pat on the back. I never reached out again, and neither did he.

I stood in the parking lot holding my box and watched the taillights of Dad's Audi as they drove away out of my life. Suddenly I got tears in my eyes, but not because of any sense of my own loss. Somehow, in that moment of separation that would impact me in ways I never could have imagined, I felt sympathy for my mother and wondered what it must be like for her to see her last child leave home. I thought it must be hard for her. I felt her sadness. However, I felt none of my own. I suppose I had a child in me that was screaming, "Noooooo!" He must have been terrified, abandoned, and alone. But I didn't hear him.

I had tuned that kid out long ago and would not give him an ear until twenty years later. For now I had a box of personal items, a new authority, and that was that. I finally had left home. I went back inside and asked Roger where I could buy a pack of cigarettes.

Shelter Care

At this point I entered a world of real-life outcasts. Every teenager I came into contact with in foster homes, shelter homes (temporary foster homes providing shelter not to exceed fifty-six consecutive days), group homes, and juvenile detention centers (jail for non-adults) was there for a reason. None of us were there for spitting on the sidewalk. Each of us, while there for different reasons and with different stories, was no longer accepted in traditional homes. We were undesirable. We became someone else's problem. The one thing each of us had in common was that we wanted to be free of authority. Some of us learned to live within the system better than others, but none of us liked it.

This "system" of child placement was like a fast flowing river. I was dropped into the middle of it and I simply did not have the tools, attitude, or aptitude to navigate my way back to shore. For the next nine months, I would move in and out of five shelter homes, two boys' group homes, enjoy nine visits to juvenile detention, and run away too many times to remember. One time I attempted to count the number of moves during this period. I came up with twenty-six.

My first stop was a shelter home in Dallas, Oregon. Those who qualified to be shelter parents were paid per day for each child in their care. I've never understood the exact set exact set of requirements for being a house parent, but I'm sure they did not include being observed in action. There were five or six of us in this home. Our only real interaction with the house parents was during meals and chores. Most of our time was spent hanging out in a small add-on living room listening to 8-track tapes.

I came in at the bottom of the pecking order, and that included male and female. I was small, about 115 pounds and posed about as much threat as a wet napkin. Out of style short hair, out of style clothes, pimples, no money, and a fairly advanced vocabulary all set me apart from the others. Almost immediately I recognized that I was an outcast among outcasts. I suppose the fact that I smoked was enough to gain a modicum of tolerance from the other kids. I quickly understood that the only way I would survive was to act a lot tougher than I was and be willing to accept any dare if it meant an increase in the coolness factor.

I was accustomed to this, however. In the eighth grade I began every day by the creek just off school grounds smoking cigarettes with the "hoods" and stoner crowd. It's safe to say I was probably the only one out there with straight A's that year. On the first day of my new life away from home I enrolled in the local high school, taking similar classes as I had taken at home. Everyone else at this shelter home went to a vocational school. I learned quickly that most kids in the system could not go to public school as they were either too far behind or simply caused too much trouble.

I went to each class only once. After the first day, I never set foot in Dallas High School again. Enrolling felt normal. Skipping classes did too. The opportunity to experience six hours of freedom was too much temptation. I'd hitchhike the ten miles back to Monmouth where I would score some weed and just goof off until school was out. This became my sole purpose in life; no one was going to tell me what to do.

It was perfectly natural to continue leading a dual life. For years I had done this at home—one life in front of my parents and an entirely different one away from them. At the shelter home I helped with the dishes without being asked, obeyed their rules perfectly, and spoke to them with respect. During the first couple of days the house parents may have wondered why I was there, but by Friday evening—just four days after arriving—there was no question.

A young Indian girl living in the shelter home seemed to thrive on attention from the boys. She would sit on the couch listening to the Ohio Players and jerk off the boy sitting beside her. I had not yet even kissed a girl and was quite fascinated by this, although I tried to act nonchalant, as if this were a common occurrence in my life. At around 7:00 p.m. I was outside smoking a cigarette when this young girl thought it would be funny to shut the door and lock it. She looked at me through the glass window and started to laugh. I snapped. Without a second thought I shattered the window with my bare fist, reached inside, and unlocked the door.

This split-second decision occurred without a single thought of consequence. I could not tolerate anything I considered unfair, especially if I were the one getting the short stick. I would have none of it. I had a right to open the door, and what she did as a silly joke actually poked what was at the very heart of my screaming child's hurt and pain: unfairness. I made it clear who would have the power now. I would determine what was fair.

The house parents' anger over my shattering their window was only assuaged by the sight of blood streaming from the cuts on my hand and wrist. But just a phone call later I was in a car on my way to Marion County Juvenile Detention Home (JDH). It would be the first of nine trips.

JDH

JDH is jail for kids. Nearly every medium to large city has one. It had all the makings of an adult jail, but without the adults. We were processed, strip searched, given jail clothes, and put in a tiny room with a tiny window in the metal door. As a part of orientation we were required to stay in that room from twenty-four to forty-eight hours before being allowed to mingle with the others. Our behavior and ability to follow directions determined the length of time before being let out. Their directions to me were "stop asking when you are getting out." I had no discipline. None. My first two days at JDH were spent in my cell.

This was my first real experience in a locked room and I did not do well considering the fact that just a week earlier I was riding my bike home from my job at the restaurant. And, just five days earlier I was at school wondering if I was getting kicked out of my home and mostly afraid that I would not be. All that, as dysfunctional as it was, was still normal to me. But being surrounded by four brick walls, the never-ending echo of noise from footsteps, voices, doors slamming, and continual piped music was my new normal. I never cried as I felt no sadness and no pain. That had been beaten out of me a long time ago. But I absolutely hated that room. I quickly learned how to kiss up and who to kiss up to in order to have extra privileges, which minimized my time behind that door.

I was finally let out of my room for breakfast with the other inmates. There were boys and girls from ages twelve to eighteen, some new like me and others already hardened by having a significant amount of time in the system. Some were there from California Youth Authority (CYA) and I heard many stories of gangs, gunfights, robberies, and the like. Most of us looked up to them, and I could only hope to someday acquire such status.

JDH also had school. Every hour I spent working on Math and English counted toward my high school diploma, something I was extremely grateful for later. I had nearly completed 11th grade and had taken advanced math, writing, and science courses. The materials provided to me were of the 7th and 8th grade levels. I realized then that although I had screwed up like everyone else in JDH, we had little in common academically. One of the teachers at this school took notice and I soaked it up like a sponge. Maybe I didn't belong there. Maybe I would find a foster home as my brother Dennis had and finish high school. Maybe.

My first of nine visits to JDH lasted only four days. Roger Mattson picked me up and returned me to the same shelter home in Dallas. The house parent was no longer loving and supportive of the young kid he'd taken in. Rather, he quickly pulled me aside and let me know he was against me coming back and would be watching me. That's fine, I thought. He was just a prick. And I was smarter than he was.

This time I lasted only a couple of days. A fifteen-year-old girl took a liking to me and we decided to run away together. We hitched a ride to Dennis' apartment in Albany, about thirty miles away. While I was in Dennis' bedroom working on getting the girl's clothes off, Dennis was on the phone with my dad. Evidently Roger Mattson, upon hearing I had run away, called my dad. My dad immediately called Dennis. Dennis made the right decision and told the truth. After all, what was Dennis going to do with two teenage runaways? So, before anything could progress in the bedroom to the point of having bragging rights, I heard a knock at my door. It was my father and his friend Tom Mesdag. While Tom and my father drove both of us to JDH, my only thought was, *Damn! So, so close!* I was still a virgin.

After a few days in JDH I was sent to a different shelter home. This one was on Center Street in Salem, Oregon and I would end up spending considerable time there off and on throughout the rest of the year. I was figuring out how to act in order to fit in more easily with society's young misfits. I especially liked this home because we spent most of our time in the basement out of sight from the house parents and staff.

We hung out with the girls, listening to music and copping feels whenever we could. The slow music of the 70s was ideal music to dance to for a bunch of opportunistic boys—"Shannon" by Henry Gross, "Color my World" by Chicago, "Wildfire" by Michael Martin Murphey. I slowly began to feel like I was fitting in, no longer an outcast.

We didn't have school in this home, but we did have library time where we would spend two hours a day in quiet time reading. To this day I am still surprised their book collection contained *The Happy Hooker* (Xaviera Hollander). It definitely was my favorite, and I hid it from the others for my exclusive use.

We had a pool table too. We'd had one in our living room at home. (Dad was a trader of everything—boats, jukeboxes, cars, tractors, tools, and even a pool table). One of the staff members looked exactly like Frito Bandito in the Lay's potato chip commercials, so much so that we called him Frito and the name just stuck. He was an excellent pool player. Although he was staff and he made us follow the rules, I felt even back then that he actually cared about us.

Sandy, the housemother, sat down and talked with me one day. I suppose we talked about why I was there and if I had any plans to change my behavior. She said something to me at the end of that conversation that I remember to this day. She looked me in the eyes and said, "I like you, Dwaine." I like you, not I love you or Jesus loves you, but "*I* like you."

I did not feel likeable. I was a screw-up, a juvenile delinquent, a pot smoker, a class skipper, a dirty book reader, a thief. How could Sandy possibly like me? Why? How could someone who knew me for sixteen years send me away, and this relative stranger said she liked me? Somehow, she saw some value in this worthless kid. Compounding this, an incident occurred shortly after that really stuck with me and actually shaped my perception of what is right and wrong.

We were not allowed to smoke in bed. These kinds of rules meant nothing to me as long as I didn't get caught. But one night I was caught having a cigarette in the top bunk shortly after lights out. I did my typical repenting, which probably included a tear or two. "I'm so sorry. Forgive me, sir. I won't let you down, sir." About five minutes after he left I lit up again. He was waiting. And watching. He came back into my room, and he was pissed. "You know what you are?" he asked. "You're a sneak. You're worse than just someone being disobedient. You're a sneak and you're a liar. There's nothing worse than a sneak."

That really got to me. I didn't mind being a kid who broke the rules, but I didn't like the "sneak" label. This is why later on in my journey I insisted on robbing people face to face with a knife or at gunpoint. I felt superior to those who burglarized an empty home.

But for now, in an attempt to gain status with the other shelter care kids, I started stealing cartons of cigarettes from a Payless store in downtown Salem and selling the packs for a quarter each. Of course, the girls got theirs for free.

As one might expect from a home that contained both boys and girls, there was a lot of fooling around and at Center Street Shelter Home there was plenty of opportunity for it. Probably due to the free cigarettes, but certainly not due to my geeky, no-muscle, pimply-faced features, I managed to have my first physical encounter with a couple of the girls there. To be honest, the extent of my introduction to the mysteries of sex was some random groping, but I felt an incredible amount of acceptance and belonging as a result.

It had been about three weeks since I was kicked out of my home when I was caught hitchhiking on Highway 22. I really don't know where I was going or why I was out there, but the police took me to JDH, and the following day I was standing in front of Judge Williams at Polk County Court House in Dallas for the third time in less than a month. This time he told me that the next time he saw me he would declare me a ward of the state of Oregon and I would be sent back to JDH to stay until they figured out what they were going to do with me. "Yes, sir. Fly right, yes sir. I'll be good, sir."

I did not understand what "ward of the state" meant, but it didn't matter if I were under my parents', the state's, or Roger Mattson's jurisdiction. I would do what I wanted to do when I wanted to do it. I was all about the current moment. "Now" was all that mattered. When I was being reprimanded I would hang my head and apologize; however, I felt no remorse. I just gave them whatever it took to get through that moment. Once away from the house, I was free. And I absolutely loved that feeling. I lived for it. I never gave a single moment of thought for the consequences of any action on which I might embark.

The very next day, the Payless drug store loss prevention finally figured out who was stealing all those cigarettes. A woman rent-a-cop caught me outside the store with two cartons of Marlboros under my sweatshirt. She had a long-legged, former-track star store employee with her just in case I felt like running.

Judge Williams was true to his word. This time I sat in JDH for a few weeks waiting for Roger Mattson to find a place where I could possibly be successful. Again, while I was locked up with virtually no freedom and very little opportunity to screw up, I earned extra privileges and had no behavioral issues. But I was still wild in my heart, and I simply did and said what was necessary to satisfy them so I could get out. I made promises to do better this time. "I'll change; I really will."

Hawthorne Manor

I was accepted into a boys' group home in Corvallis, Oregon called Hawthorne Manor. I had no idea what it was or how much freedom it would allow, but anything was better than jail.

By the time I walked up the front porch stairs of Hawthorne Manor, school was out and summer had arrived. Just a few houses off the corner of 9th and Van Buren, it looked no different than any other house on this street, but there were about ten male juvenile delinquents living in this home who had broken at least one of society's rules. All of them were deemed deviant and incorrigible. I sat in the office with Roger and Tom, the home's director. Tom was looking over my paperwork, which included my scholastic transcripts.

"So you have been going to public school?" Tom said with an eyebrow raised.

I was prepared for that statement. "Well, they say I'm super smart," I replied with feigned humility.

"No," Tom responded pointedly. "You may be smart." He hesitated for effect. "But I'm super smart."

And the game was on.

The house was two stories tall plus a basement. All the boys' rooms were upstairs, two to a room. I shared a room with a longhaired boy named Aaron who had the look of a heavy metal rock and roll star. I met a few of the other boys—Wade, Joe, Ray, Gary—all of whom were older and much cooler than I was. I was still five foot nothing and barely weighed a buck thirty-five. There would be no testing from this group—I was no threat.

Within a few hours of my arrival I demonstrated my immaturity by sharing how I would be supplying the guys with cigarettes that I would steal from supermarkets. I believed that information would not be shared with staff. I immediately learned a hard lesson that "snitching," like beauty, is in the eye of the beholder. My self-declaration as the house cigarette supplier made it to the office staff before dinner. The boys used this as an immediate opportunity to solidify their positional hierarchy with the house staff by snitching me out. I had a long way to go before I would figure out how to play this game. A few weeks later I informed the staff that Gary had been drinking at a party. I was called a "tattletale" by house authorities and written up. Gary got the knowing look and the wink by the staff member. I was labeled and ridiculed by the other boys as a snitch. You would have thought I committed high treason. It wasn't fair; but that's just the way it was.

My first priority was to find out how much freedom I would have. Hawthorne Manor had instituted a tiered system: Levels 1 through 4. Beginning on Level 1, I would be allowed to leave the house with another resident for short periods. Level 4 allowed the resident to come and go as he pleased. I would never make it to Level 4. Or Level 3. Or even Level 2.

Most of the guys had jobs in construction. I worked in a daycare for $2.50 per hour until a child told me that his mother spanked him. When his mother came to pick him up, I confronted her in the middle of the street and threatened to beat her ass (I believe those were my exact words). I'm not shocked at my reaction considering my own upbringing, but I did not understand why I was fired. It was the pecking order—I figured I was near the bottom but slightly above an abusive mother. The woman agreed not to press charges for my threats.

Losing the job was disappointing because it offered me a chance to get out of the house, but all we cared about then was getting high and finding a party. Corvallis, Oregon is a college town and nearly every block seemed to have a party on Friday and Saturday nights. While we were not invited, we had no issues with helping ourselves to alcohol and weed until people began to question who we were. Even then, we might be allowed to stay. Often, if we arrived after the party was over, we would finish whatever was left in the bottles.

One day I met some hippies who invited me into their house to get high. They pulled out a cigar box filled with marijuana. After enjoying their generosity, I snuck back later when the house was empty and unlocked and I stole that cigar box and nearly two ounces of pot. Excited, I decided to share my find with one of the other Hawthorne Manor residents. He just took it from me. I had watched him beat up an old man earlier and I wanted no part of it. Easy come; easy go.

As another way to access free alcohol, I stole cases from beer trucks that were unloading their stock at a super market in downtown Corvallis. It's amazing how often I got away with it. One day the driver saw me and I managed to run off without getting caught, but it scared me enough to cease my exploitation of this method for obtaining alcohol.

One night I went out with one of the guys, and we stopped at a mom and pop store in downtown Corvallis. I shoved a bottle of Red Lady wine down the front of my pants and walked out of the store, unseen. As Joe and I walked away we suddenly heard some yelling, "Hey, stop! Stop that guy!" Running out of the store was a hippy with a bottle of Mountain White Chablis in his hand. As he ran past us, Joe took off, quickly catching him and tackling him to the ground. He held him there while we waited for the police to come and arrest the thief.

After the police left, Joe and I walked to the high school and made our way to the top of the football bleachers to share our stolen bottle of Red Lady. I had had a drink or two before—just enough to feel tired—but this was different. This was my first drunk. That night I experienced what it was like to have the ground come up to meet me, hitting me directly in the face. I ended up at a party where I could not walk without falling down. At one point I tried to pull myself off the floor apparently by grabbing a large girl's crotch, which upset the men in the crowd. I don't know if I got up immediately or simply went to sleep on the floor, but at some point I made it back to Hawthorne Manor. I walked in through the front door, battered and bleeding from my forehead. The incident was logged and I was informed once again that I was on restriction.

The next morning I woke up with my face bruised and with scratches all over my body. I was sore from head to toe. And yet, all I could think was, *I want to do this every day for the rest of my life.* I was an alcoholic from my first drunk. I had an allergy to alcohol that manifested itself as a craving for more. And it would be an obsession of my mind daily from then on.

From the first time I went on restriction to my last day, I would never have any real privileges during my stay at Hawthorne Manor. I never moved off Level 1 and spent nearly all of my time on restriction. Restriction meant we were required to stay in the day room. The intent was to inflict boredom as a punishment. It worked. But I found a way around the restriction that had no worse consequences. I would go out the window of the day room and search for a party and a place to get high. Eventually I'd come back through the front door, stoned and drunk. They would log an incident and I would be placed on restriction, forced to spend all day in the day room, with the open window. And on and on it went.

At some point I was allowed to attend church. I had grown up actively attending the Wisconsin Synod

Lutheran Church and was confirmed in the 8th grade. I also had been playing the organ for the services since I was twelve years old. I believed what I was told was true. There was no reason not to. I was a sinner and I was going to hell. But I would take any opportunity to get away from the house.

I was asked to play for the church services and practiced all week for the upcoming Sunday gathering. The house had an upright piano, which I played frequently. That first Sunday I played well enough that the pastor asked me to play again two weeks later. That was the plan. Only, the Saturday evening prior to my performance, I went to a party, stayed out late, and was still significantly inebriated on Sunday morning. When it came time to play, I sat down at the piano and hit about three or four notes. They were the wrong ones. I was immediately ushered out of the church and, not surprisingly, was not invited back.

Amazingly I had only one physical altercation at Hawthorne Manor, and it was certainly well deserved on my part. One day one of the guys who owned a pet rat was gone from the house for the weekend. We had been drinking and I thought it would be an excellent idea to shave Ray's pet rat with an electric beard trimmer. Ray returned and was extremely displeased. The rat was now mostly skin with some tuffs of hair here and there. I sat on the edge of my bed, waiting. It was only a matter of time until he came for me. When Ray came in I could smell the alcohol. I stood up and his left fist found my groin. As I doubled over his right fist landed directly on my nose. I briefly saw stars and my eyes instantly watered. Another resident and opportunist, Wade, lifted my head off the bed by my hair and busted my lip for good measure. I didn't like it, but I also knew that this was life in a boys' group home.

At some point during the summer, the state police caught me hitchhiking with a large amount of speed. This was a class-B felony and put me in a completely different category with the state. I was no longer just incorrigible. I was a sixteen-year-old convicted felon.

I was surprised that Hawthorne Manor put up with me as long as they did. I enrolled in high school after the summer but never went to a single class. A friend who had been in the house now rented a room that was conveniently located on my way to school. We spent many days just taking bong hits, listening to Aerosmith, and playing along with the guitar.

Finally, after I ran away again for nearly a week they gave up. Tom was hoping his "super smartness" would be my saving grace, but he realized whatever it was that I needed would not be found at Hawthorne Manor. Tom called Roger and once again I was in the back of a car on my way to JDH.

Hawthorne House (The Janus Program)

Just five months after I left home I felt like a veteran delinquent. I never feared getting caught and had no fear of consequences if I was caught. After a few days in JDH I went to the notorious Van Wyke's house in Aumsville, Oregon. We spent all of our time in the garage unless we were shoveling horse stalls for cigarettes. The second night at this shelter home another kid and I snuck out and stole an old pickup from a nearby farm. Having grown up in the country I knew most farmers rarely took the keys out of the ignition. We drove it around for a few hours and put it back, close to its original location. The next day Roger dropped by and took me to another shelter home so far into the country that even if I were to run away, I'd never be able to find my way out.

After a couple of weeks I received word that I was accepted into a drug and alcohol program in Portland, Oregon called the Janus Program. The residence was called Hawthorne House (completely unrelated to Hawthorne Manor). It was on the corner of 39th and East Hawthorne—thus, the name.

Had Roger Mattson or the Hawthorne House staff understood the extent of my self-esteem issues and undeniable drive to be free from authority, they might not have agreed to place me in a large city like Portland. It didn't take me long to see that it had everything I wanted in order to hide. Even walking the ten blocks to school felt like freedom to me.

In order to be able to go to public school and not vocational school, I worked hard at convincing the staff I wanted to change. It worked, at least enough that they let me enroll in Cleveland High School. Until now I had only gone to small town schools with no more than 500 students. Cleveland had thousands. Also, there were as many African Americans as there were Caucasians.

The first day I went to each class. After that I only went to my Guitar class first thing in the morning. I actually even got a grade out of it. The rest of the time I did whatever I could to get high, which proved to be much more difficult as I still looked like I was twelve. More often than not after asking if a group of kids had weed, the response was "Get out of here, narc." And they'd all laugh. There was no sense in arguing; in fact, I can't blame them. I still didn't fit anywhere. Not with the tough crowd. Not with the smart kids. I never made a single friend at that school and became very comfortable with walking the suburban streets of Portland alone. After school was out I went back to the house. "How was school?" they'd ask.

"Fine."

Within just a couple of weeks, the staff was notified that I had not been attending school. I stood in front of them as they lectured, feeling much like I did when I would stand in front of my parents. While they were going on and on about the virtues of honesty, I made the decision in my mind to leave Hawthorne House. The next morning a couple of hours after school started I doubled back. The house was vacant, but locked up tight. I broke a window in the back door, let myself in, and grabbed some clothes and my stereo system. I took the bus downtown and pawned my stereo for $35.

Feeling rich, I took a bus back to Cleveland High School to try and buy a lid (one ounce of pot for $10).

I'm not sure why I thought it would be safe to get into the back seat of an old impala between two dark-skinned strangers. But, within ten minutes of doing so, they helped themselves to all of my cash. I asked them if they would be so kind as to leave me some bus change. Somehow I was going to have to sharpen my street smarts or this would get old really quick.

Emancipation

On the run again, I hitchhiked north on I-5 and ended up in Olympia, Washington. I hid in the shadows, as I was sure every policeman in Oregon and Washington State was looking for me. I liked the feeling and excitement of being on the run. Somehow it made me feel important. It did not occur to me that I was just another kid walking down the street, waiting on a corner for a walk sign.

It was November 1976 and I turned seventeen. Barely more than seven months had passed since I was waking up at home, fixing my lunch, and taking the bus to school. l had been learning abstract math and history, acting in my drama class, and playing the organ at church on Sunday mornings. Now I had no idea how I would get my next meal or where I would stay at night. And I did not have a single regret.

I received a free rent voucher from a church that I could use to stay at the Angelus Hotel on 4th Avenue. I had never felt so domestic. I had never felt so grown up. I even got a job at the China Clipper restaurant washing dishes and peeling onions. I made some drinking friends, one of whom had a guitar. I worked, had a place to live, ate, drank, and got high daily. I felt as though I'd arrived at maturity. I was finally all grown up. If mom and dad could see me now, they would truly be proud of me.

After a couple of weeks I called Roger Mattson with an idea. I said I would like to come back to Salem, but I wanted to be emancipated. Emancipation was a significant word for those under eighteen in the juvenile system. It meant freedom. It meant I would be legally on my own, not a runaway or in a boys' home. Roger said he would try, but I would still need to return and spend some time in JDH first as a consequence for running away from Hawthorne House in Portland.

I took a bus back to Salem, did my requisite week in JDH and went back to the shelter home to wait for a court date. I got a job washing dishes at the Tahiti Restaurant. No longer was I the new kid in the shelter home. I was nearly an adult! The other kids looked up to me, especially because I had a job. The staff at Center Street shelter home treated me with a newfound respect, and a couple girls liked me. The awkward, insecure kid had been replaced by a confident, mature young man.

During this period I met Donna Marcus while drinking coffee at VIP's restaurant in Salem. Donna would be my first, rendering me no longer a virgin. I was truly all grown up!

Finally, Judge Williams signed the court papers allowing for a "trial emancipation." I had four specific mandates to abide by for six months. If I did that, I would become an adult legally. The rules were:

1. Keep residence at the YMCA;
2. Keep job at the Tahiti Restaurant;
3. No alcohol consumption;
4. No use of drugs of any kind.

I didn't make it. In fact, within three weeks I had lost my job, lost my residence at the YMCA. I had vomited one night all over the bed and never returned. I drank to excess nearly every day, and I nearly overdosed on pills and alcohol six times (three requiring visits to the emergency room).

Why was I unable to comply with a few simple rules? I didn't stand a chance. I had no coping skills. I was on a road that led only to self-destruction. My direction was to anywhere other than success. I was acting like I felt—devalued, worthless, a failure.

Roger Mattson picked me up and took me in front of Judge Williams one last time. They were left without any options. There was no other viable choice. I was sentenced to be incarcerated at MacLaren School for Boys in Woodburn, Oregon.

Roger drove the twenty miles from Dallas to Salem, returning me to JDH where I would stay until the paperwork had been completed. As we crossed the Willamette River, we were stopped in traffic about ten cars from the red light at the end of the bridge heading into downtown. I jumped out of the car and ran as fast as I could, heading for Donna's house. I didn't want to go back to JDH or MacLaren. I liked my freedom. I was happy.

Later that evening after one last rendezvous with Donna I knew I needed to turn myself in. Part of it was guilt. I liked Roger and I felt guilty for running away from him. He had never done anything purposeful to hurt me, and in an odd way I knew he had some level of care for me. I would find out later that Roger was a man of faith and he prayed for me. Often. But for this evening, it was a ride back to JDH. I was on my way to MacLaren.

MacLaren School for Boys

MacLaren is a notorious institution with a long history of abuse by staff and other inmates. More than once while growing up I heard: "Keep that up and you'll end up in MacLaren." Located just outside of Woodburn, Oregon it was the home for hundreds of kids, ages ten to twenty, who were simply unable to abide by the simple laws governing reasonable social interaction. Some of our country's most famous criminals have passed through MacLaren, one of the most notable being Gary Gilmore who was eventually put to death in Utah. Ann Rule provides a little more detail about Gary's incarceration, specifically the decision to put him on Thorazine. This drug was a control tool for managing the most violent inmates, because it made them extremely lethargic and they were unable to do much more than just sit and stare. Their desire to be combative was severely diminished. Anyone on this drug was labeled a "ding" by the rest of the inmates and staff. I had close contact with many dings before I left MacLaren.

This time Roger left nothing to chance and I was transported from JDH to MacLaren in handcuffs. Turning off Highway 99, we drove the long road to the administration building. The boys' reformatory looked rather benign, but I wasn't fooled. There were eight housing units, four on each side of the road. These were called "cottages" with names like Dunbar, McBride, and Kinkade. I never learned why, but I assume it was a meager attempt to paint the institution as a rehabilitation center. Each of these units contained about thirty boys and enough staff to keep an eye on almost everything, but not completely as I would soon find out.

Just past the admin building were the galley (food service), gymnasium, higher security "cottages," and finally the "R" Units. One of these R Units would be my home for the next thirty days. As the R might suggest, these were the receiving units, broken down into two sections: one for those who were returning for breaking parole and the other for first-timers such as myself. The time spent in the R Units allowed for mental and physical evaluation and to determine where the new inmate would best fit in main population.

I quickly discovered that my main source of concern was not the other boys, but the staff. They were mean and did not put up with any lip from mouthy, punk kids. Since most of us were mouthy punk kids, a number of us were literally punched in the face without hesitation and without warning. Possibly due to a military influence, if one of us screwed up, all of us were punished. One of the staff's favorite forms of punishment was to get all of us up in the middle of the night to make and remake our beds. If a quarter did not bounce sufficiently on a bed, we had to rip off the bedding and do it again.

But no staff member was as mean as the one we called "The Red Ant." We called him that because of his red hair and fiery temper. He was only five and a half feet with an obvious little man's complex. I believe he went to work hoping for an opportunity to punch or kick a boy every day.

Later during my time there, karma got the best of the Red Ant, and it was completely his own doing. In the middle of the reception compound was a ball field where we played softball on Saturdays. Often the staff would play as well, and on this day the Red Ant was up to bat. He took a pitch deep into left field and tore down the baseline. Rounding first base on his way to second he decided to stretch it into a triple. A funny thing happened though half way to third: His right hip pocket began to smoke, and as he stepped on third base with a stand-up triple, his stupid grin suddenly turned into a grimace as we all watched bright orange flames shooting out from his right pocket. The Red Ant was literally on fire. He screamed (like a little girl we would later embellish), threw himself on the ground, and rolled in the dirt in a complete panic.

The Red Ant smoked a pipe and kept his wooden matches in his right pocket. Somehow the friction of him running the bases lit one, then another, and finally all of the matches caught on fire causing smoke, flames, and much to our delight, burning flesh. None of us could stop laughing then or even later that night when we were again learning to make our beds the right way. All we had to do was think of him screaming with his backside on fire. It couldn't have happened to a better man.

After two boys' homes, countless shelter homes and nine visits to JDH, I had learned how to do time, both mentally and socially. I was barely 135 pounds and never really learned how to fight. So my best asset was my ability to speak and, if nothing else, completely confuse the aggressor so he walked away scratching his head, not knowing if I had backed down or if he had just been insulted. I was scared to fight though and worked diligently to avoid finding myself in that position. Fights at MacLaren were nearly a daily occurrence. Some kids jockeyed for prestige by picking fights with smaller kids. Winning those fights was not always a foregone conclusion. More than once the skinny, freckle-faced kid had taken years of boxing lessons and put a pretty good whipping on the bully.

There was one occasion in the chow hall that left me somewhat exposed. A fight broke out in the table next to us and it ended up with one of the kids thrown on our table. The staff immediately broke up the fight, but a minute later when I tried to take a bite of scrambled eggs, my fork was shaking so badly that the food fell off before it could reach my mouth. This did not go unnoticed and brought a few laughs from around my table. I felt foolish, and it surprised even me.

I know why I reacted that way. I had been at the mercy of a violent and angry man for as long as I could remember and had suffered countless beatings at the hand of my father. From early on until I was fourteen I would lie down on my bed and my father would beat me with a board, often freshly cut from plywood due to the previous one being broken on me or my brothers. When he felt I was getting too old for this form of punishment, he would simply grab my throat with one hand and slap my face with the other. I can still see him, his face red with rage and shaking, his finger pointing at my face just an inch away.

I think I was always scared of the other boys just as I had been of my father for my whole life. But just as I did at home, I learned how to navigate relationships and, for the most, part stay away from the bad guys.

Finally I had been processed, categorized, and assigned to Dunbar Cottage. Dunbar was closest to the highway on one side of the entrance road. I can assume those deemed least likely to run or "hike" were eligible for this housing unit. A cottage consisted of a dorm with at least thirty single beds. There was a large day room with tables for playing cards, a pool table, and TV area. It had a bathroom/shower area called the "flats" and a small kitchen and dining area. In the middle of all of this was a staff cubicle, including a glass office and door for the cottage manager. Our manager was seventy years old, but he was a tough old codger and you knew not to mess with him. We were allowed to have our own clothes, but they also handed out basic necessities like jeans, t-shirts, underwear, and such. Knowing who was supported by family and who was there basically on their own was easy based on the clothes they wore. I had nothing of my own.

Within the first week at Dunbar I was enrolled in school. And this time, I went. First, I had no choice and, second, I would do anything to get out of the cottage every day. They determined I needed very few credits in order to get a high school diploma. They also made it very easy for me. A packet of English or Math equated to a week. Eighteen weeks equaled a full credit. When I left home almost done with my junior year I was taking Algebra II. At best, the math packet contained work required for pre-algebra. English was no different. There was also reading and history, but it was all very simple.

This institution was no different from the boys' homes I lived at in that it also had a level system called "tags." They used colors—white tag, red tag, yellow tag, and green tag. There was even "extra green," which you could only receive if you were selected. The minimum amount of time on each tag was two weeks and by the end of two months I was on the green tag.

It seemed that the more structure I had the easier it became to follow the rules. I exceled under the structure and discipline without any negative marks against me. At "extra green" I got to hang out with the cool kids in the kitchen. We got to eat snacks and stay up late. The boys in the lower levels looked up to me.

By mid-June 1977 I had achieved enough credits to graduate from high school. And as a bonus, my parents picked me up for my first "home visit." Home visits were overnight stays away from MacLaren and were the highest privilege a juvenile could receive.

The home visit did not go well. My parents still lived in the same house as when I left. The next door neighbor girl who previously had not given me the time of day suddenly seemed interested in the juvenile delinquent on a home visit from MacLaren. In the small trailer home in their driveway I had her pants halfway off when her dad opened the door. Her father took exception and told my parents how he felt about their son coming home from a boys' prison attempting to fornicate with his daughter.

I set a time and location for Sunday to meet my parents in Salem to take me back. It did not even occur to me to spend any time with them. I found Donna, my former girlfriend, and figured out pretty quickly that she had moved on. I got stoned and felt the first bit of freedom in nearly six months. My parents picked me up at the appointed time, and the drive back to MacLaren was mostly silent, other than dad telling me this would not happen again. He was right. That would be my one and only home visit.

Chapter 2
A TURN FOR THE WORSE

Four boys graduated that year from William P. Lord High School, MacLaren School for Boys, and I was one of them. I was proud, considering I had been to five different schools since I left home just over a year earlier. My mother came to the ceremony and I did have tears in my eyes when I was handed my diploma. Early on I had taken my education for granted, but came to recognize the value. I had assumed all kids knew the Pythagorean Theorem and how it would apply to the distance formula. Sentence structure and grammar came naturally to me, something I learned in the 6th grade. While my grades suffered due to non-attendance, I was fairly sound academically.

My ability to articulate well, however, became a detriment and was beginning to put some space between the other boys and me. During cottage meetings even the staff accused me of using big words on purpose just to show I was better than others. Back then and even now I have to wonder just how smart one had to be to work at MacLaren. I never did this on purpose; it was just my way of communicating. It's all I knew.

I began to feel the itch—the same itch that came up every time I ran away from shelter care and boys homes. When my counselor and I discussed my leaving MacLaren and becoming emancipated, she voiced her concern about my drug usage and alcohol abuse. In short, she said no. Since the day I left home, I did not take "no" well, especially if I thought I was in the right. I didn't have a drug problem. Well, as far as I was concerned, they couldn't prove that I had a drug problem since other than my home visit and sharing some pot brownies one time I hadn't taken drugs in six months. I certainly had not drunk alcohol. It was my life and I was sick of people telling me what I could and could not do.

There were no fences around MacLaren in the summer of 1977. There were security cars called "ODs" that roamed the perimeter. Sometimes guys would attempt to hike, but were almost always caught. One day shortly after the conversation with my counselor, Pastor Ed asked me if I wanted to join him on a visit to a convalescence center in Woodburn. He was the protestant pastor at MacLaren and had heard me play hymns on the piano in the administration building.

I agreed to go and decided that I would take off and run the first chance I could. On the afternoon of June 28th after we arrived at the center I sat at the piano and began to play from the Lutheran hymnal. I really liked playing for people who enjoyed listening, and more than one elderly resident sang along with "Sweet Hour of Prayer" and "Just as I Am." But when Pastor Ed said he was going visiting, I was out the door before you could say "How Great Thou Art."

I didn't know where I was; I just ran as fast as I could once I got out the front door. I quickly learned the direction to the highway and within fifteen minutes I was on the side of I-5 under an overpass with my thumb out. Back then hitchhiking was legal on the highway in the state of Oregon. I got a ride almost immediately and I breathed a sigh of relief. I had escaped from MacLaren. I had no thought of the consequences, no plan, no clothes, no money, and I didn't care. I was free.

Just thirty miles south of Woodburn I looked up an old friend of mine in Salem. He was a cook at the Tahiti Restaurant and had taken me under his wing during my trial emancipation period. I didn't know what to expect from him and had not put much thought into the trouble he could get into by harboring a fugitive. He let me stay at his apartment that first night and kindly told me the next morning that he could not help me other than to give me a little money for food. Even with my immaturity, I understood.

I hitchhiked to Monmouth-Independence. My parents had moved to Tigard near Portland, and no one was aware that I had escaped from MacLaren. I sponged off friends the best I could and was able to make any story believable—just passing through town on my way to some job somewhere worked particularly well. I was very good with adults for one or two days at least. It was the 4th of July and there were plenty of group picnics in parks to meet people and have free food and free booze.

I also discovered another way to survive: girls. I was seventeen, my hair had grown out, and I looked enough like a bad boy that I could easily draw attention from the teenage church girls. For a day I could make believe whatever I wanted and have a place to stay, food, pot, alcohol, and if I was really lucky, reach third base. But I was never comfortable with maintaining a lie for very long and it was better for me to stay on the move.

There was one young lady I knew from high school who was a couple of years older than me. She bought whatever story I told her and even let me use her car. Other than stealing a few cars when I was in shelter homes I had very little driving experience. One day I drove her car south out of Monmouth on Pacific Highway and was stopped by a state trooper for speeding. I figured that was it; I was caught! I had no drivers' license, so I gave him the name of my older brother Danny. I signed for the speeding ticket and he let me drive away. It was just my lucky day.

Feeling as though I wore out my welcome, I hit the road with my thumb out. I could survive simply hitchhiking from one place to another. Drivers nearly always gave me cash and I just acted the part of a young guy sowing his wild oats. I also learned quickly that hitchhiking could be dangerous. Very dangerous.

On my way south I got picked up late at night by a middle-aged guy in an old pickup. I got a weird vibe from him from the beginning and was especially concerned with the fact that the passenger side door would not open, so I had to enter from the driver's side. But, a ride was a ride, so I took the chance. We were only a few miles down the road when I felt his hand creep over to my leg and land on my left knee. I ran through the possibilities in my head within just a few seconds and decided my best option was to act violent and crazy, figuring he would be afraid and let me out. My plan worked. He slammed on his brakes and got out. I followed him out of the driver's side but was suddenly frozen in fear when I saw the knife in his right hand. I will never know his intentions, whether he had drawn it for his protection or something else. But I took off, running into the night as if he was chasing me every step of the way. I ran until I was too exhausted even to walk.

The next day I was picked up in Southern Oregon by an Asian man who seemed harmless enough. I was glad to be able to get a long ride all the way to California by someone who looked like a typical, middle class white-collar worker. I put the seat back and drifted off into a deep sleep.

When I woke up it took me a few seconds to get my bearings. I was in a car, riding down the highway. My jeans were unbuttoned and my zipper was down. A hand was where my zipper should have been. This guy was having free rein with my junk. I guess the pent up anger and frustration of my life surfaced at that moment, and without considering the possible consequences of beating up the driver of a car while speeding down a highway doing 70 mph, I unleashed a whipping on him. I turned toward him and slammed my fist into the side of his head over and over again. How he managed to pull the car over safely and stop on the side of the freeway is a mystery to me. I'm quite sure his face had numerous broken bones as my knuckles were cut and bloodied. And even though I was angry, I felt vindicated. I felt as though my actions were righteous. I felt good. Really good. This was my first act of violence and I had not even a hint of remorse.

In all I was on the run for three weeks. I met a Christian girl at a music store in Redding, California and I confided to her the truth of my escape from MacLaren. She suggested that God would want me to turn myself in. I didn't like that idea at all. But she was cute and I actually thought that she liked me. Maybe even cared about me. That night I had a run in with the police at the local park. I had stolen a prostitute's car and she pointed me out to a police officer who chased me through the park. I got away, but the next day I thought about what the girl said. I went back to the music store and had her call the police. I did it for her. In my mind, she would like me more if I did it. This is how low my self-esteem was. I turned myself in to be liked. I spent the night in jail and the next day two security officers from MacLaren drove down to Redding, shackled my wrists to a chain around my waist and put leg irons around my ankles. I was going back to MacLaren. If I thought things were bad when I left, they were about to get a lot worse. Significantly worse.

Welcome to DSS-1

Detention Special Services 1, DSS-1 or D1 as it was usually called, is the jail inside of the jail. And of all the jail and prison cells I have been in (and there have been many), this was truly the worst of the worst. It was late July and somehow the heat found its way in, but could not find its way out. The stone walls literally sweated day and night. I was given pajama-like bottoms and top, a blanket and a roll of toilet paper. I used the blanket to wipe the sweat from my body, which was constant. The door had a six-inch by four-inch window which was so dirty it did not provide much of a view. I began to second guess my decision to impress the girl in Redding.

We were allowed out of our cells for about thirty minutes a day to do jumping jacks and other calisthenics. We took a shower every other day. Meals were delivered in a paper bag—usually meat between two slices of dry bread and an apple. That was it. The only enjoyment any of us looked forward to was masturbating at least three times a day. At least I had privacy instead of doing it secretly at night in a dorm room with thirty other boys.

I was sent back to Dunbar cottage after a week in D1. I could tell immediately that things were different. First, I was on White-Tag restricted. That meant I had to sit on the bench that lined one side of the day room whenever I was not sleeping, working, or using the flats. I had at one time been Extra Green-Tag—the top of the mountain, respected and admired. Now I was the loser sitting on the bench. To make matters worse, the staff was hard on everyone after my successful escape, so the other boys were going to make it very hard on me.

The second day out of D1 I got slugged on the back of my head. I knew the guy who did it. A huge kid. He didn't say anything, just gave me the "What are you gonna do about it?" look. I did nothing. I felt so defeated. Some of the boys who previously saw me as one of the leaders made crude remarks and laughed behind my back. I was like a wounded animal. Everyone felt free to take a shot at me.

One of those boys was Chris Quisenberry. Chris and I had been good friends, both of us with high privileges living the good life before my escape. He had been an amateur boxer on the streets and although I had never seen him fight, I somehow believed that he could hold his own. One morning as I was sitting on the bench waiting to go to my job in the galley, he walked by and punched me in my face, splitting my lip. Again I did nothing. Later that day, I told a friend of mine about it—a guy I had lived with previously at Hawthorne Manor in Corvallis. He felt that retaliating was my best option, but I needed an equalizer. Bon Ami® cleanser was such an equalizer—lye soap. I filled my jeans pocket with the white powder.

It was a long walk back to Dunbar cottage. I had the powder in my pocket. I was determined and there was no going back. I walked through the front door and straight into the kitchen. Chris was sitting in a chair at a table with his back to me signing a greeting card. Sitting across from him was Scott Cavilee, his best friend. I did not hesitate. It played out to me like a slow motion scene in a movie. I walked to Chris's side and turned toward him, putting my hand in my pocket, and grabbing a handful of the powder. At the same time, Scott began to rise, suspecting something was up, and saw the powder in my clenched fist. I called his name.

He looked up. Scott yelled "Nooooo!!," but it was too late. I threw the handful of Bon Ami cleanser directly into Chris's eyes and I began to pummel him about his head and face with my fists. Chris jumped up, bringing his hands to his face and screamed loud enough for the other cottages to hear, then fell to his knees. Arms from behind pulled me back and I shook them off and walked to the office. Chris no longer had eyelashes or eyebrows and his face was bloody. I don't know how long it took for him to see again. As I sat in that office, nearly all of the rest of the boys were yelling their threats through the office window. The old manager looked at me and said "I've got a good mind to send you back out there." Not for grace but to keep his job, he called security and I was ushered back to D1 in an OD car.

I felt great about what I had done. He deserved it. There were no rules that applied to a boys reformatory fight. I spent another week in D1—another week of sweat, isolation, loneliness, bad food, and self-gratification three times a day. There was some excitement this time from the daily doldrums. One of the other boys, Don Brakke, managed to break his toilet which flooded all the cells. I was able to see the staff drag him out of his cell and spray him with pepper spray. Don just laughed. The intense heat and sweat literally prevented the spray from getting into his skin pores. So, in a simple and matter of fact manner, the staff dragged the laughing kid into the shower and turned on the cold water. Within seconds he began to scream. I covered my ears as it had somehow lost its entertainment value.

I can understand now why MacLaren was the subject of so many lawsuits since 1960. Even in adult prisons there was some consideration for separating inmates who had violent histories toward each other, but not at MacLaren. I couldn't believe I was sent back to Dunbar. Chris was still there and his eyebrows and eyelashes were now just stubs. I still had to sit on the bench. And this time instead of punching me in the face, Chris sat beside me and said very calmly, as if he were talking to his best friend, "Here's what I'm going to do. I'm just going to break your jaw. That's it. Just your jaw. And you won't know when it's coming." And he got up and walked away.

Okay, now I was scared. I had always managed to keep myself relatively safe, but I felt my luck had run out. It reminded me of when I would do something wrong, serious enough for my dad to tell me to go upstairs when we got home and lay down and wait. I had thrown lye soap in this kid's face and he had all the reasons and justification to take his revenge. There was not a soul in the building who would lift a finger to help me. I was on my own. There was nowhere to go. Nowhere to hide.

That morning I went back to work in the galley. For work, we changed out of our clothes into white pants and a white shirt in a locked, caged room in the galley basement. I purposely put my clothes as close to the edge as possible where I could reach them through the bars with my skinny arms. At around two in the afternoon, after the staff had eaten, I went to the basement, reached into the metal cage and retrieved my jeans and shirt. I quickly took off the whites, put on my street clothes and put the whites back on over them. I worked a broom back and forth, shuffling backward until I reached the mop closet in the corner of the cafeteria. I stepped in, took off my whites, and slipped out the back door unseen.

I ran. I ran as fast as I could, although I was in an area completely foreign to me. I ran past what looked like rows of strawberries being picked by Mexican migrant workers. They lifted their heads and watched me fly by. I saw some tall Douglas fir trees ahead of me in a gully surrounded by a dirt road. Luckily, I grew up in the country and had been climbing trees since I was seven. It didn't take me long to get nearly to the top of one of these trees. This gave me the vantage point where I could see them coming long before they got to the tree line. They could see my footsteps in the dusty road going into the gully, but they did not see them come out. They knew I was in there somewhere. Finally they walked into the trees and brush, slowly, methodically, taking a step at a time expecting to find me hiding behind a bush or tree. I watched the whole thing from my position in the top of that tree, and had they simply looked up, my story would have taken a different turn and I might have been saved from a demoralizing, debilitating future. But they did not look up. After about two hours, they finally gave up. I stayed in that tree for at least another two hours thinking they would be coming back. When they didn't, I cautiously climbed down and walked until I found a main road. It was the beginning of August, 1977. And I was on the run again.

The Dirty Streets

There is a whole other world that exists in large inner-city streets that you won't notice unless you know what to look for. To the average person, it is unseen. A man and woman talking in front of Penny's on 2nd and Pike in Seattle, Washington could be a father inquiring into his daughter's recent department store purchase. Another man driving around the block multiple times might simply be lost, and his conversation through the passenger window with a young man at the bus stop might simply be to ask for directions.

But those who thrive in the darkness know the true nature of these rendezvous. They are sordid transactions, each with its own value proposition. Services and compensation are negotiated by both parties that, when executed, erode any remaining decency from their souls.

On one side of this transaction are average people who can be found anywhere. They are your neighbors—

professionals, white collar and blue collar workers, truck drivers, computer programmers, pastors, teachers, gay, straight, bi-sexual, traditional, weird, kinky, and some absolutely beyond imagination—and they are predators. They all have in common the untamed need and unquenched desire for sex.

On the other side of this agreement are individuals who are more difficult to find. They are the broken—lacking in self-esteem, hating themselves and their own bodies, willing to accept and dependent on financial payoff for abuse, self-degradation, demoralization, and mental and physical pain, addicted to drugs and/or alcohol, in need of food, cigarettes, and a place to sleep—and they, too, are predators.

When these two entities meet and make an exchange, every angel in heaven and on earth cries. God must cry too. It was not what He intended. In the end, whatever dignity that was left is lost. Any sense of remaining civility, justice, or goodness to life slips away, further eroded by the human condition—unfiltered, unstopped, and unchallenged.

But the result is conveniently omitted by the marketing agents of the street. It is presented as a red carpet to happiness, security, and love. It is the lie that keeps the cesspool in operation—an oasis for those who are lost and longing for nurturing. It is a magnet to anyone on the fast track to self-destruction. Yet, it is simply a mirage.

The first enticement dangled in front of them is acceptance. Those who are agents of the darkness prowling in the daylight are more than welcoming to the new souls, the desperate runaways. There is no judgment, only acceptance, family, friends, and love. Although I liked to think I was experienced, I was fresh meat for these veterans of the street to prey on.

Three important events occurred in August of 1977. The first Star Wars episode was released, Elvis Presley died, and I wandered into this world and became a male prostitute.

It's not an easy thing to divulge. I thought long and hard about leaving it out of my story. It's still embarrassing even after nearly forty years. I decided to share it because it was a critical choice made by a kid who was hurting profoundly. It was a conscious decision made out of revenge to get back at a mother and father who rejected him. And at the end of the day, it was the only apparent option for a boy on the street in need of money.

I had been hanging out at the Seattle Center with a guy who was trying to teach me how to burglarize houses and cars at night, but I wasn't very good at it. One day a couple of teenage girls, friends of his, and I were getting high at the Center and they started talking about "hustling" at Penny's Corner for money. Twenty, thirty, forty dollars, and more for fifteen minutes of work. I assumed they meant some kind of con game.

When I pried further they explained it was prostitution and they made it clear it was not older women and young men. It was men on men, or rather, men with boys.

I don't know why I was not repulsed by this. Perhaps it was because I felt I would be the one in control. Maybe it was simply the money. But I think it was most likely the fact that someone wanted me and was willing to pay for it. In my world, that incredibly odd and false sense of value woke up a deeply hidden, quieted part of me that longed for attention and love and meaning. The girls filled me in on what to do, where to go, how to stand, and what to say. I hopped on the monorail, got off on 5th and Pine, and walked the few blocks to Penny's Corner to sell my body and my soul.

I arrived at a bus stop on Union Avenue between 2nd and 1st Street and waited. I wasn't nervous about getting in a stranger's car as I'd done it so many times before while hitchhiking. However I was concerned and uptight about what I may have to do.

On his second time around the block a man driving a Lincoln Continental slowed down. He was obviously looking me over. Was I a cop? Would I just beat him up and rob him? Was I young enough? Old enough? He sped up and moved on.

On his next pass he slowed and motioned to an empty parking spot on 1st Street, drove to it, and parked. I crossed the street and looked around. I don't know why—I wouldn't have known how to spot an undercover officer unless he had a badge and a handgun in his holster. I opened his car door and climbed in. He did not fit the stereotype. He could have been a superior court judge. After he introduced himself he got right down to business and asked, "How much?"

"Forty," I responded.

"I have twenty five."

"Forty," I stated again.

"I'm sorry, that's too much," he said sadly.

I hopped out of the car. I was disappointed; but, if I were to do this thing it would be on my terms . . . or so I thought. I walked around the block and ran into the two girls. I quickly learned my first lesson on street hustling: people exaggerate. If a hustler said she got forty dollars per trick, it meant she got paid forty dollars one time. The other times were much less. The girls educated me on this and scolded me for not accepting the offer. Back to the corner under the bus stop.

It took less than five minutes to get picked up again. This time I agreed to thirty dollars and we talked like we were old friends as he drove me to Volunteer Park in Capitol Hill. We got out of the car and walked in the darkness down one of the well-used dirt paths. We hunkered down behind some bushes and the event occurred. It was disgusting. It was demeaning. I felt like a garbage disposal and I swore I'd never do that again.

The john returned me to Penny's Corner thirty dollars richer. I found the two girls and did what I could to wipe it from my memory: purchased some liquor and pot and a room for the night at the Savoy Hotel on 2nd Avenue. We found a 24-hour restaurant, ate, returned to the hotel, and Angel and I had sex. The money, food, booze, and pot were gone by midnight so I walked the two blocks back to Penny's Corner and was picked up almost instantly. It was too easy. Just too easy.

It also opened up a whole new world. I fell in love with the street life instantly. I made friends quickly. Girls wanted to sleep with me. Guys wanted to hang out with me. Somehow I transitioned overnight from a geeky, pimply, out-of-place little kid to a street kid everyone wanted to know. It was my first experience with popularity on the street. I turned heads, male and female.

I met a taxi driver and his girlfriend who let me stay in their hotel room about four blocks north of Penny's corner on 1st Avenue. They had rice, curry, a cooking pot and a single burner for heating water. I ate lots of rice and curry, and to this day the memory of that hotel room comes rushing back when I taste those flavors.

They also happened to be the main source for the influx of a popular street drug called Mescaline into Seattle. It is made from Peyote and gives both a mind and body high.

During the day we would hang out at the Donut Shop owned by Gunther Manholt that sat kitty-cornered from the famous Pike Place Market. Gunther befriended the street kids and would always give me a cup of coffee and a donut if I didn't have the money to pay for it. Gunther was arrested in 1981 for using street kids, and his own son, to burglarize homes and businesses. I also heard rumors that he made kids prostitute for him, but I had never seen that and I question if it is true.

Our days consisted of passing the time until darkness came. We lived for the night. We felt like we owned the streets after dark. I would pull a quick trick to get money for drugs. Next we would go to the disco, either The Association on 2nd Avenue and Union or Aquarius in Pioneer Square. These were alcohol-free, drug-fueled disco establishments where the only reason adults frequented them was to look for underage kids to exploit. The Association had a back room with no tables and chairs, just pillows on the floor. In short, these places were cesspools with sharks and little fish who stood no chance. And I loved it. I had never felt so connected.

I had good friends: Cameron, who was also on the run from a boy's institution; Angel, who liked me best when I had cash; and red-haired Carol who I would later hook up with in Portland. But the combination of drugs and alcohol with emotionally and mentally disturbed kids on the run is an especially volatile cocktail, which meant friendship could turn into animosity without warning or logical reasons.

One Friday night we were walking around Pioneer Square, high on a mixture of Mescaline, Valium, and alcohol. Cameron, Angel, and I found ourselves walking in a back alley where we encountered a bum stumbling around with a dirty green bottle of wine in his hand. In an effort to impress my friends, I started taunting the old man, calling him names and pretending I wanted to fight—the first of many bad choices I made that evening under the influence of a dangerous cocktail. I had never seen anyone move that fast, least of all a drunken bum. Before I could blink he smashed the bottle against a concrete slab, wrapped his left arm around my neck and pressed the jagged edge against my throat. He said, "Give me a reason why I shouldn't kill you."

"Because I was just kidding. I was joking around, I didn't mean it. I'm really sorry. I really am." My voice shook with terror, "Please sir, please let me go."

He did. I don't know why, but he did. We walked the ten blocks or so back to my hotel room. Soon after, Cameron suddenly grabbed a knife and began chasing me all over the neighborhood. I don't know what I said to set him off, but I was running on rooftops, fire escapes, alleys, etc. just trying to get away from him. At some point he forgot why he was chasing me, but I was still wary that his memory might return, so I took a long kitchen knife from my room and left.

By then the sun was coming up, so I walked down by the water of Elliott Bay. I felt bad about myself, partly because I was coming down hard off the Mescaline and also because two people had come close to killing me in the last few hours. I saw a lady in her fifties walking toward me, clutching a large purse in her right hand. I reached behind my back and grabbed the handle of the knife I'd been carrying. When she came within just a few feet of me I pulled the knife out and pointed the tip of the blade right at her stomach. With my other hand I reached out and grasped the strap of her purse and said as menacingly as I possibly could, "Give me your purse, lady!" How quickly the victim becomes the aggressor. I had never robbed anyone before. I expected this lady would let go of the purse and I could run to a safe place to count the treasure.

It did not play out that way. This lady said "No!"

I was at a loss. I didn't have a manual with directions on how to respond to a lady with a knife pointed at her stomach who still refused to give up her purse. I certainly was not about to stab her. So I began wrestling with the purse strap, trying to rip it out of her hand. After a brief struggle, she finally let go and said, "Here, take it, punk." And with that, she turned and walked away.

Demoralized and demeaned again, I went back to the hotel room and emptied out the contents of the purse. There were about fifty pennies and a tampon. I wasn't so sure I was cut out for robbery. I was refused, rejected, and called a punk by a woman who risked getting stabbed for a half dollar and a feminine hygiene product. In addition I had been chased for hours and nearly had my throat cut.

I was no longer the innocent kid standing in a parking lot with a box of stuff, watching his parents drive away, leaving him to be someone else's problem. Breaking a window at a shelter home and getting sent to JDH now seemed distant and relatively harmless.

After about a month of living my new crazy life in downtown Seattle, I found myself on Penny's Corner at three in the morning. By now most of the patrons had cleared out for the night, which left just me, an old beat up 1968 Biscayne rumbling around the corner, and some low fog drifting in off Elliott Bay. The car's muffler rattled loudly and the coughing and sputtering engine echoed off the buildings. When he went around the first time we eyeballed each other, like both of us knew at that moment neither of us was the cream of the crop. He sped up and drove around the block for another pass. This time he went by me about thirty yards and parked, leaving the engine running. I looked around for police and, not identifying any, walked up to the car, opened the door, and got in.

He was old, ugly, and unkempt in every possible way. His face was grotesque. His clothes were as dirty as the seats of his car. He smelled putrid. As he spoke he seemed to be trying to smile, but I doubt he'd had much success with that in many years. You could not tell where his gums stopped and his teeth began.

"How much do ya want?" he asked.

Understanding basic street economics, I knew this

would not be a landfall. It was that last negotiation of the night. I responded, "Twenty."

He also understood basic street economics. It was 3:00 a.m. He was the only customer. And I would not be out there if I had a penny to my name. The foul man countered, "A place to sleep, a shower in the morning, and cigarettes."

I'd be lying if I said I didn't think about it. I was exhausted and had no money or cigarettes. But as tempting as his offer was, I opened the door and got out. I just couldn't do it. As I heard him driving away I was already walking toward the I-5 southbound onramp. I stuck my thumb out and quickly caught a ride to Portland, sleeping soundly the whole way.

Back to MacLaren

It didn't take me long to find the hustling area of downtown Portland where the street kids hung out— just a few blocks from the Greyhound bus station on 3rd and Yamhill. It was Saturday night and there was lots of activity. I found the same acceptance from the street kids in Portland that I had in Seattle.

I secured a place to spend the night and a ride the next morning back to town where I was dropped off in Old Portland. It was around 7:00 a.m. when I crossed the street and was quickly surrounded by three police cars. Some of the officers had me face the wall and patted me down while a couple others investigated the tavern on the corner. Apparently, unbeknownst to me, just a few minutes before I arrived on that corner, a silent alarm in the bar had accidently been triggered.

The police apologized and let me go. Unfortunately, however, I had given them my real name. I had taken only a few steps down the block when I heard their radio crackle, "Dwaine Casmey is an escapee from MacLaren School for Boys." It must have looked pretty funny to see me try to outrun police officers in three-inch disco platform shoes. I made it about five steps before I was up against the building wall again. Only this time, in my frustration, I jerked my right arm away when the officer attempted to put it behind my back to handcuff me. I was immediately sorry for that decision. I had no idea I could reach the top of my head from behind my back.

I was placed in a holding cell and two security officers from MacLaren picked me up the next day. I spent two days in D1, and then was assigned, yet again, to Dunbar cottage. This time, thankfully, Chris was gone, ending that saga.

But things were different. I was different. I had just spent four weeks living a life that was so far from anything I had experienced before. I tasted it. I loved it. And I could not wait until I could go back to it.

Also, while I was in Seattle, I called my father and told him what I had been doing. At the time I was rather matter of fact about it. I did not consciously divulge that to hurt him—I could barely consider what I felt, much less what someone else might feel. However, subconsciously, I obviously had an agenda. I found out later that it impacted him enough that he ended up in the hospital. Years later, in therapy, I would smile at that.

But now, back in MacLaren, I was just numb. I didn't care about gaining levels, but I wasn't intent on rebelling either. I went through the motions of whatever I was told to do, but very disengaged. I knew I did not belong there. I belonged on the streets with my new friends.

Just one day after returning to Dunbar, I was sitting on the bench in the day room, serving my time on restricted White Tag for the escape. A young gay kid sat by me and put his hand on my leg. I grabbed it and pushed it off, saying nothing.

He went back to a table where I saw one of the other inmates whisper something in his ear. I was not aware that the inmate had told him I actually liked it and to do it again. This time, when the kid sat by me and put his hand on my knee, I commenced to rain blows on his head and face with my fists. I remember feeling nothing—not anger, not fear, not compassion . . . nothing. This was the last day I would spend at Dunbar cottage and was sent back to the hole late that evening.

DSS-2

The remainder of my time at MacLaren was spent in Detention Special Services 2, or D2. While D1 was the highest security *detention* unit, D2 was the highest security *housing* unit. It butted up next to D1 in the same building. The only reason ever to be outside was a trip to the hospital, and the inmate would travel in handcuffs and leg irons. Every inmate movement was planned and controlled. If we were sitting down we asked to stand up. If we were standing we asked to sit down.

The housing unit contained a small day room, a TV room, a dorm room with about eight beds in addition to four individual open-door rooms and a flat (restroom/shower). I would spend the next four months in this small area with about eleven other inmates.

There were two specific programs for D2. The first and most common was an 8-week program. In order to leave D2 the inmate simply had to have eight good weeks, and not even in a row. Each week the staff evaluated the inmate as to whether or not he did what he was told and whether he met their basic behavior requirements. If so, that was one good week. One of the guys in D2 had been there for a year and a half. He still had not successfully completed eight good weeks. The second program was simply a six-month term as punishment for bad behavior.

All of the inmates in D2 were there for a reason,

something I discovered the first week. Of over 500 MacLaren residents, these twelve were considered the worst of the worst. Even though I was definitely not the toughest or the biggest screw up, they had simply run out of options. And since I did not fit into either program, they just placed me in D2 until I was legally emancipated. Since my eighteenth birthday was November 12th, just two months away, it was only a matter of paperwork and signatures.

There were a couple of guys who seemed to be extremely lethargic. They did what they were told, but were not communicative. They were doing what we called the "Thorazine Shuffle." They were kept medicated for their safety as well as the safety of staff and other inmates. We called them dings.

The same kid who busted his toilet in D1 managed to avoid taking his medication for a couple of days. I thought he was great. He was extremely funny and happy-go-lucky. But when the staff realized he was no longer taking his Thorazine, they called for backup. I didn't realize at first what was happening. But this vignette had been played out many times before. Don walked into the TV room, went into the far corner, and began arranging the chairs in such a way that he might be able to throw at least two of them before they could reach him. The head staff member spoke in a slow, calm, and deliberate voice as he and six other security officers inched closer and closer to Don. Don had a chair in each hand, and I could tell this was not their first dance.

As if perfectly choreographed, Don heaved the first chair as the staff and officers rushed him. There would be no opportunity to throw the second chair and it was over as quickly as it started. Seven large men subdued Don and dragged him by his ankles down the hall to D1 where he would stay for a week or so and return, head down, feet shuffling, eyes dead. I saw this scene repeated with him and others nearly weekly for the remainder of my time in D2.

Eventually I made a few friends and had no trouble earning my way to top privileges. There was only one benefit to achieving this status in D2, especially as a short-timer. It was being able to sleep in one of the four individual rooms. Shame had long since flown out the window. And based on my month in Seattle, I had very few remaining personal boundaries. But, masturbation and talking about masturbation in D2 was discussed openly and was as common as discussing what was for lunch. The allure of a private room was in having one thing that was private.

We did not have church services in D2, but there was a group of Christians that visited from Eastside Foursquare church in Gresham, Oregon. I was happy for the conversation to help pass my final weeks at MacLaren. Although I had the maturity of a twelve-year-old, I had the ability to communicate with someone beyond my years, and I enjoyed just sitting and talking with adults. I'm sure my repeated attempts to impress them were not as subtle as I hoped, but I believe I exhibited the possibility of rehabilitation, at least to them. The religious volunteers who came were hoping to be a part of a success story, and I exploited this at every opportunity.

I did find ways to use my time productively. I was able to practice typing on a manual typewriter and I spent time creating budgets and sharing with the staff how I would get a job and make ends meet when I got out. I actually believed it when I said it. But when I was alone with my thoughts and dreams, I knew I would not be taking the typical career path of most of their graduates in food service or at a gas station. I knew I would be back on Penny's corner.

In December, the paperwork for my emancipation landed on Judge Williams's desk. This is the same judge I'd seen since I'd left home and the same judge who sentenced me to MacLaren. Any day I would be getting the word that the paperwork was signed and I could walk out the door. Unfortunately, it was also Christmas time and Judge Williams was on vacation until January. There was nothing I could do about it but sit and wait until he returned after the holidays.

Jim Johnson was the inmate who had been in D2 for over eighteen months because of his inability to make the 8-week benchmark. He was sentenced to MacLaren for kidnapping a woman who picked him up hitchhiking and went straight to D2 upon his arrival. Earlier in the year the staff actually allowed him to spend a few weeks in one of the cottages hoping that would provide the necessary incentive and motivation to change his behavior. But Jim purposely got into a fight. He just didn't like it outside of D2 and as a teenager was already severely institutionalized.

I never considered myself friends with Jim and, like any reasonable human, being did what I could to avoid him. But one night shortly after lights out I heard the unique, sickening sound in the room next to mine of a fist hitting flesh. There was no crying out or even a grunt since the first punch took his victim from sleep to unconsciousness. The kid had fallen asleep face up and Jim Johnson walked into his room and simply began punching him in the face.

I knew I was next. I knew he didn't like me simply because I did well and I was soon to get out. As I quickly jumped from the bed to the floor I heard scuffling and shouting. Two other kids had tackled Jim. One of the momentary heroes had him secured in a Full-Nelson. The staff member on duty was helpless as he was locked in a cage with a view of the dorm room, but was not allowed to enter without backup. He could only watch. As I stepped out of the room Jim's eyes met mine. They were full of rage and hate, like a caged animal just waiting to get loose. All he said to me was, "You were next." He went into D1 and I never saw him again, but it took me a long time to forget those crazed, animal eyes.

Finally, on January 5th, 1978 I walked out of D2. I was given a bus pass and $60. They dropped me off in downtown Woodburn, Oregon at the Greyhound Bus station where I caught a bus to Newport, Oregon, a small town west of Salem on the Oregon coast. Dad was working there at the time and staying at a Best Western Hotel with my mother. The only stipulation for my release was to check in with my parents. It seems silly now, but I'm assuming it was a formality. I spent the night with them, but I can honestly say I do not remember anything about the twelve hours or so I was with there. I do recall it being awkward. The next day they gave me $100 and said goodbye. I walked out the door of their hotel room with a suitcase, around $150, and the full knowledge and understanding that I was finally free. It was the first moment I could choose what I would do when I wanted to do it without being on the run.

As I headed for Portland I could think of only one thing to say. Screw 'em. Screw them all.

Chapter 3
WHERE IT ALL BEGAN

I was the third of three boys born to Richard and Martha (Dalldorf) Casmey. Dennis, the oldest came May 21, 1956 and Danny arrived August 6, 1957, and I arrived on November 12, 1959 while we were living in Santa Ana, California.

My dad, Richard (Dick) Earl Casmey was born in Longview, Washington in 1936. His father, Earl, was a severe alcoholic and divorced dad's mother, Peggy, when my dad was very young. Peggy married a man named Lonny who, as I understand it, often thought he was still fighting in Korea.

Growing up as a child in Rose Valley, Washington, Dad was considered by his grade school teachers to be academically slow. He was often put in slow learner group with kids who struggled in Math and English.

The truth was that they just knew little about dyslexia back then. Had they identified it and understood how to solve this learning disability, my dad might very well have been in the head of the class. Instead, they called him stupid and told him he would not amount to much. This haunted my father for years and was the driving force behind his incredible desire to succeed and excel.

Lacking good parenting, my father found himself without any real structure. As a teenager he was that iconic bad boy—the good looking kid leaning against the 1950 dodge wearing blue jeans and a white t-shirt with a pack of camels folded into the shirt sleeve. He stole cars and got into fights. Finally, he was faced with the choice of ending up either in a boy's home or enlisting in the Marine Corps. With his mother's signature, he joined the Marines before his 18th birthday. This decision helped form an identity that he carries with him to this day. The structure of the Marine Corps provided my dad with exactly what he needed.

At some point during Dad's enlistment he met my mother, Martha Dalldorf, at a dance social in Southern California. I believe for both of them it was love at first sight. Soon after they met, my dad found himself in jail. The details are sketchy and it's not really my story to tell. But my mother bailed him out and dad decided then never to drink to excess again. With my mother's sense of loyalty to him and her determination to provide him with whatever he needed, I believe my father simply no longer felt the need for alcohol.

My mother's life prior to meeting my dad is largely unknown to me. Her biological father died when she was twelve and her mother remarried. She did very well in school and got her Secretarial Science certification. The possibility of my mother falling for the handsome, rebellious tough guy seems so unlikely given what I know of her, but she did and they were married just three months after they met.

I believe my father felt challenged by every male with whom he came into contact, so having three boys in a sense was a cruel joke. My father was absolutely determined that his three boys would not take his same path. Since he found the structure he needed in the Marine Corps, he decided this same structure would be his parenting model. And it would start early, as soon as we were old enough to say "Daddy," we were taught to call him "Sir."

In 1965 we moved to Stayton, Oregon and then moved again a year later to Scio, just outside of Stayton. We lived in a white house on top of Rollercoaster Hill (Cole School Road). It was there in this house that my story really began.

As a young child starting the 2nd grade I could not think of a cooler place to live. Acres and acres of wheat fields stretched behind our house and to the north. We made our playground in the acres of forest to the south. My brothers and I built forts and climbed Douglas fir trees. There were always new discoveries like the old one-room school house just down the hill that had burned to the foundation. The hand pump still provided water that we used for our garden in the summer. Our house and land were owned by Curt Kersniski who lived at the bottom of the hill. He was eighty years old when we rented the house from him for $30 per month. He married for the first time ten years later and died shortly thereafter.

We had a cellar where we stored firewood for the wood stove that was our only source of heat. It also had just one bathroom downstairs off the kitchen. The front porch faced east, allowing a generous portion of the morning sun to illuminate it and the huge oak tree in the front yard. My parent's bedroom was downstairs. And there was a large bonus room with two bedrooms at each end. One was long enough for three single beds and had two large windows facing the front yard. Danny and I shared this space when Dennis was old enough to claim the back room as his.

Even though this wasn't technically a farm, we really worked the land. Over the five years we were there we had three steer, four pigs, about fifty chickens, and every stray dog within ten miles. Every year we would buy a truckload of wood that needed to be chopped and stored in the basement. I learned how to cut kindling at age six and still have a scar on my left index finger from learning the hard way to let go of the wood before the hatchet came down.

Dad worked in the metal industry and we always seemed to have a nice-sized heap of scrap metal behind our house. I lost count of the times dad felt it needed to be moved to the other side of the backyard. Of course, now I realize this was how he was able to take his Saturday afternoon nap without being bothered by three boys.

In the summer we had a large garden that always seemed to require weeding. Eventually my parents purchased five acres about a mile up the road, so Dad bought a tractor to help with the maintenance. We spent many weekends setting a choker around Scotch Broom plants, pulling them up, and burning them in huge bon fires. There always seemed to be some work to do, but when Dad was satisfied with our progress, there was time to play in the forest or throw the football or baseball around.

The many strawberry and pole bean fields in that part of the country provided us with the ability to earn money to buy our school clothes. Dennis and Danny started almost immediately; I had to wait until I was eight. I still remember Dad saying if we didn't make enough money to buy our own school clothes we'd go to school naked. He was probably joking, but I believed him, of course. I believed everything my dad said. And he never joked about work.

Each of us had a homemade, single-speed bike made out of scrap metal. There was very little countryside between Stayton, Scio, Lyons, and Crabtree that we did not cover while riding our bikes. We rode to and from the strawberry and bean fields. We rode while searching for bottles and cans to return for a penny apiece. But most of the time, we just rode to get away.

If we took a right out of our driveway we were immediately challenged by the sheer height, depth, and grade of Rollercoaster Hill. The trick was to gain enough speed going downhill to coast as far as we could uphill on the other side. We lost to gravity every time much earlier than we would have liked and had to dismount and push our way to the top. Each of us lost control at least once on the way down and earned significant road rash filled with tar and asphalt as our reward.

Rollercoaster Hill was so steep that our driveway became a common turnaround for many who were not brave enough to challenge it during the winter. Getting to the top of that hill was not, and would never be, easy.

While we were not rich by any means, we weren't poor either. We never went without a meal. I do remember one time using wires in place of shoe laces, but I thought nothing of it. Every Sunday we put on our city duds and drove ten miles to church in the big city of Salem, Oregon. We had been going to a Missouri Synod Lutheran Church in Stayton until someone decided to allow the congregation to remain seated during the liturgical reading of the gospel message. The instructions in the hymnal were to stand and on our last Sunday in that church our family stood while everyone else sat as the pastor read the Bible passage.

The next Sunday we were introduced to the more conservative Wisconsin Evangelical Lutheran Synod Church (WELS) in Salem where they followed the liturgical instructions in the hymnal to a 'T.'' My brothers and I would go through two years of confirmation before being allowed to kneel at the altar and receive the Communion sacraments. Many years later I attended a church where the communion cups and wafers were distributed to the congregation together in the pews and I fully expected we would all suddenly burst into flames.

We had a piano and eventually an organ in our living room and I had special musical abilities at a very young age. I learned how to read music on my own by locating the black dots on sheet music and the corresponding keys on the piano and understood the bass clef from playing trombone at school. I was never afraid to demonstrate my talent in front of a crowd at special events. I started playing the organ for church services when I was eleven when the pastor's wife and church organist went into labor. I quickly learned the songs for the upcoming week and ended up sharing the responsibility with her for the next five years.

Dad always had a board position along with his best friend, Bob Blair. The first couple of years the services were held at a Raggedy Ann Day Nursery, but in 1974 we purchased property and built a church. Going to church, VBS (Vacation Bible School), Confirmation, and potlucks were as much a part of life as going to school. I don't ever remember my family missing a Sunday. I believed the stories in the Bible and assumed that was enough to get me into heaven.

More than once I heard other parishioners and adults mention how well behaved my brothers and I were. This is how our family looked from the outside. A hard working father, a loving, quiet mother, and three good, very well-behaved boys. Nobody knew that anything other than perfect behavior had serious consequences.

There were many things that occurred in that old white house that nobody knew. Punishment was severe. It's hard to put the right word to it. "Spanking" is an understatement; "beating" conjures the image of being pummeled with fists, but that wasn't his method until I was a teenager. Instead, whatever the transgression, Dad would tell me to go upstairs and wait. Waiting was the hard part, because I knew what would soon transpire. When I heard the table saw start up in the basement I knew he was preparing to saw off a fresh length of 5/8" plywood, three or four inches wide. When I could hear the buzz of the saw silenced and his footsteps on the first floor landing, I began to tremble. I then would hear the back door open and shut, which was my mother stepping outside, presumably so she would not have to hear what came next.

My father's footsteps became clearer and louder as he ascended the staircase to the second floor where I would be waiting, lying face down on the bed. Dad had to pass by my baby pictures on the wall of the staircase and I wonder now if he ever turned his gaze the other way. I suspect it didn't matter and was not likely part of his ritual.

My tears would start as I heard the heavy plodding as he crossed the room. the instrument of punishment rhythmically tapping his right leg. More often than not he would question me, "You asked for this, didn't you?" as he made his way to me splayed out on the bed. With his six-foot frame he loomed high over me and raised the board above his head. Then he would command, "Move your hands." I always started out this way, with my hands covering my backside as if this simple act of protection would somehow prevent the board from hitting me. He would command again, "I said, move your hands!" And I would.

I do not know the degree of impact experienced by other kids in other families during "spankings" or "whippings," but my dad was rock solid with muscles from the Marine Corp and years of blue collar work. And he used all of that to bring that board down hard on my backside—hard enough to leave welts and bruises. It hurt. It hurt badly. And I cried. Every time. And after each occurrence Dad would say the same thing before he left: "Quit crying, or I'll give you something else to cry about." I would stifle myself long enough for him to leave the room, and I learned how to cry into my pillow so he wouldn't hear it.

The same punishment occurred for each offense, but the number of times the board landed depended on the severity of my crime. The reasons for his discipline were many: deviation from any instruction, failing in tasks, not completing them within the designated time, or not completing them at all, forgetting to feed the dog, moving around too much during the sermon at church, stealing a cookie.

I remember one time in particular when we received an especially brutal lashing. It was winter and we had no heat at night. The house was heated by a wood stove downstairs and , and rather than running to the only bathroom in the cold, my brothers and I got creative. There were cracks in the wall we used for such a purpose. Sometimes we opened the front window. On occasion I used a shoebox and Dennis used a shoe. One day my mother was investigating a foul odor and discovered the blackened, yellowish streaks behind the dresser. That was my doing. During that particular whipping I was in my pajamas and socks. After it was over and Dad had left, I looked down at my feet. The white sock on my left foot was crimson red. I had kicked my feet during the event and the corner of the board had cut a dime-sized gash on the top of my foot. Mom was gone, so I found Dad outside and showed him the bright red, bloody foot and the blood drained from his face. He took me inside, cleaned it up, and put a bandage on it. I could tell he was concerned, but there were no apologies that day. There was never an apology for any discipline inflicted on our family. But I knew it bothered him, and I felt some vindication in that.

The beatings were frequent. I remember one period when Dennis received a beating every day for thirteen days in a row. Often, all three of us were the recipients together. One evening Mom and Dad said they were going over to their friends' house to play Pinochle. We were already in bed when they left, and as soon as the car tail lights were out of sight we did what we usually did. We had fun. We all ran downstairs and played pee war as we urinated simultaneously into the toilet. We laughed and punched each other. Dennis opened the refrigerator and upon noticing the nearly empty pie plate he yelled, "Man, Dad ate all the pie again!"

I grabbed some snacks, left the kitchen and headed for the stairs. I said, "Hi, Dad."   He was standing there with his arms folded.

Dennis and Danny were still in the kitchen, but Danny said "Ha ha, oh sure!" When he stepped into the living room, he simply stopped and stared.

For a moment Dennis still thought it was a joke. But when he came around the corner and saw Dad, he just hung his head and moaned softly, "Oh no!"

Dad simply said, "Get upstairs." Soon we heard the table saw running in the basement. When he came upstairs, I was first. When he came to Danny, Danny refused to move his hands, so Dad brought the board down anyway. Danny jumped up screaming and dove headfirst over my bed, landing between the bed and the wall.

Dad yelled, "Get up!"

Danny shouted, "No!"

Dad reached over and hauled Danny back to his bed, laid him over his lap, put one leg over both of Danny's calves and held both of Danny's hands in his left hand, leaving his right hand free to wield the board. Danny was helpless and Dad eventually broke the board into pieces on his backside.

But he wasn't finished. Dennis still had his coming. The table saw started up twice that night.

There were many times when my brothers and I colluded as to who would take the punishment for a an infraction we committed together. For instance, if we threw the football around the living room and broke a lamp, we would discuss whose turn it was to take the beating. I have to admit that Dennis and Danny took the fall for me more than once. While it is common in some families for siblings to do the typical finger pointing, we did the opposite. Only once did one of us tell on the other two.

We lived with the constant threat of this form of punishment. Often Dad's orders would come with the not so subtle reminder to do this or "I'll blister you so you won't sit down for a week." It is no exaggeration to say that I was scared of my father for as long as I can remember. I was terrified. If he asked me to do something and I moved too slowly, he would jump out of his chair, point his finger right at my face and say, "Boy, you run when I tell you to do something! Do you hear me?"

There was one occasion when we were chopping wood when he said, "You can't do anything right, can you?"

I disagreed. Very softly I said "No, sir."

He drew his right hand back, his face turned red and he started to shake.

"Yes, sir." Agree, or be hit. It was an easy decision.

Dad was at work during the day, so Mom had the day-to-day responsibility of raising us, and we did not make it easy on her. As scared as we were of dad, we pushed our mother to the limit. And when my mother would hit her breaking point whatever was in reach would suddenly become airborne—salt shakers, glasses, utensils, knives. We learned to hit the floor and cover up.

Sometimes mom would sit on one of us and try slap our face. It was fairly easy to keep her from connecting while laughing the whole time. Finally we would let her get in a couple of solid hits and she would stop, as long as we were able to keep from laughing. If not, even a giggle would continue the onslaught.

And as was often the case, Mom would utter the words, "Wait until your father comes home." We knew what that meant. I would beg her to change her mind. I cried my apologies, to no avail. One of my favorite pleas was, "Mom, don't you love us?" It was so hard for me to understand how my mother could report my bad behavior when she knew the inevitable result.

With all the changes and healing in my life today, it is still difficult to comprehend how my mother could stand by while her three boys were the victims of abuse over and over again. One day when I was around seven she did pack all three of us up and put us in the car. To this day I still do not know the circumstances that prompted her to consider leaving with us. I often wonder what would have happened if she had actually driven off. But, she didn't. It was the only time as a child that I was aware of a disagreement between my parents.

Conversely, one day when our pastor was visiting I overheard their conversation. Mom said to the pastor, "We beat them and beat them and beat them again, but still they can't get it right." So, while I liked to think of my mother at times as a victim as well, that statement was proof enough that she supported the form and severity of punishment.

Another form of discipline used was a method Dad hijacked from one of Dennis's 7th grade teachers. Dennis had misbehaved at school and as a result was told to write a five-hundred-word essay that described why the behavior was wrong. Dad really liked that idea and would often use this same method of punishment on the weekends. I believe that it was mainly to avoid having us interfere with or intrude on his downtime. I always felt that my father tolerated us hanging out with him and Mom, but his preference was that we were out of sight. When we were forced to write long essays, we were not allowed to do anything else until it was finished, and it could take a long time to write 3,000 words on why I should remember to feed the dog.

Then there were the rules that simply did not make sense at the time and still do not make sense today. Some of them had to do with food. We were always required to finish everything on our plate. That is not necessarily a bad thing in that it promotes a healthy attitude regarding waste. However, I absolutely hated soggy cereal. Too much milk with too many corn flakes will simply take the crunch out after just a few minutes. But that bowl of remaining soggy mess would be waiting for me when I got home, and it had to be eaten before I could eat dinner. One time Dennis did not finish his cereal before we drove to Seattle, Washington on a day trip. The cereal came with us on the trip. We all ate lunch and dinner at restaurants, except Dennis. He just stared at that bowl. Finally, when we got home late in the evening, he managed to finish it.

But one of the oddest experiences I had relating to finishing meals happened to Dennis and Danny. Dad made a habit of asking us if we finished our school lunch and my brothers made the mistake of telling the truth. They did not touch their cottage cheese. Dennis and Danny absolutely hated it. My dad despised it too, so much that he couldn't stand the sight of it and wanted to vomit just looking at it. But, for dinner, Dad made my mother dish out a bowl of cottage cheese for each of them. They had to eat it under the threat of a beating. Danny ate some, but Dennis just stared at it until my father made his final threat. Dennis took a curd on the end of his fork and slowly put it into his mouth. A second later he jumped up, ran into the bathroom gagging. My father roared with laughter and Dennis took the beating.

In the 4th grade I was picked on by a kid named Norman. He would chase me and make fun of me as I was very small for my age and always looked as though I should be in a lower grade. I learned early on that there was a pecking order and one day I simply had had enough. As he chased me down the hallway out I stepped to my left, put my right foot out to trip him and shoved Norman hard, sending him sprawling down the hall until he hit a wall. I hit him about his head and face with my fists and felt the rush of adrenaline and power. It made him cry. Nearly every time I saw Norman after that I would hit him. Finally, after bloodying his lip with my fist one morning at recess, Norman cried and asked, "Why are you always hitting me?" I felt so bad because I didn't know why I continued to hit him. I apologized and we became good friends after that. I had been seeing my father looking at me through Norman's eyes. I wished I could ask my father, "Why are you always hitting me?" But I was simply too scared.

So this was the life we had for my first six years of school. We navigated waters of play, hard work, and brutal punishment. We never looked at our dad in the eye for fear that he'd feel challenged, so we took it out on our mother. Mom looked the other way and seemed completely detached after she informed our father of daily disobedience.

We all did very well in school. Dennis and I seemed to be naturally gifted academically, and Danny did as well but with more effort. Danny had been the only one to deny Dad, but was beat senseless as a result, so he simply stopped screwing up.

Dennis, on the other hand, started smoking cigarettes. He was caught, of course, and was sent to the Wisconsin Synod Lutheran Church (WELS) seminary prep school in South Dakota for his freshman year. I never figured out if it was punishment or a reward. I would have taken any opportunity even at the age of eleven to leave home if I could. But Dennis was sent home just a few months later, kicked out for smoking and drinking.

When Dennis returned I followed him out to the forest one day to watch him smoke. Dad smoked like a chimney, probably two packs a day. I'm sure Dennis was stealing his cigarettes. I wanted to try it, and I did. Even though I didn't inhale, I thought I was the coolest kid in the world. When I did inhale I coughed my lungs out, but only the first couple of times. I was addicted the moment I tried it.

Just a month or so later Dad took Danny into town to pick up some building supplies. When they returned, Dad got all three of us together to retrieve some of the boards we had used to build forts in the forest to add to his supply. We poked around a couple of places, then ended up in our main fort area. Danny stood on the two by eight board that covered a hole in the ground where we kept our cigarettes. I was hoping this would prevent Dad from using that particular piece of wood. Unfortunately, Danny was identifying it as our cigarette safe. Dad flipped the board over and the pack of Marlboros loomed large as the center of attention.

Dennis said something for which Dad kicked him in his leg so hard that he fell to ground in pain. Dad marched Dennis and I upstairs. That beating was particularly severe. And that's the way it would be until I left home. I smoked. I got caught. I was punished. And I smoked again.

I was mad at Danny for some time for ratting us out, but at the same time I knew he was no match for Dad. Danny had learned to stay out of danger. But he also shut down emotionally, a trait I believe aided him later as an officer in the Marine Corp.

After sixth grade we moved a few miles away to Lyons. It had a population of under 1,000. We purchased a house right behind the fire station for $12,000. I loved it because it was also next to a lumber mill with ponds that contained catfish and bluegill. I also loved the idea of a fresh start. We had lots of freedom to go fishing in the Santiam River and mill ponds, ride our bikes around town, have a paper route, and basically have excuses to be away from home for long periods.

Parents who worked in the mill had to be strong, and by extension their kids grew up tough as well. The eighth grade class had six boys and six girls. Seventh grade, my class, had a new teacher fresh out of college. I liked him because he would cuss sometimes and drove a 1970 Plymouth Barracuda. I thought he was cool. My mother did not agree and made every effort to report him to the school board as often as she could.

I entered adolescence during this time and did not do well with it. I was okay if I was alone. But around classmates, adults, people at church, and virtually anyone else I was extremely self-conscious and felt like I did not fit in anywhere. Just a year earlier I would have been happy playing monsters with my friends, but now I just wanted to be alone and listen to Neil Young sing "Heart of Gold" or "Old Man."

I decided on my own to ask the teachers and my classmates to call me "It." Many agreed, at least for a while, including my teacher. I felt comfort in being nondescript. The school counselor asked me why I

87

wanted this, and although I cannot remember the reason I gave her (it was probably "I don't know") it was good enough for her. She said "Okay!," smiled, and that was that. Eventually the novelty wore off and everyone went back to using my real name.

Because of my size and the fact that it was a tough town, I was picked on. Mostly I was made fun of. There was one particular kid named Danny who saw me as just under him in the pecking order. I was able to ignore it most of the time. But one day during choir he sat behind me and changed the words of a Karen Carpenter song to "Dwaine's a slug. He's a little sloppy slug . . . ." I felt perfectly calm and in control, but something in me snapped and I also felt a red hot fiery ball of rage in my gut. I got up, walked behind him and put him in a choke hold. With my free arm I began to punch the side of his face and head with my fist. It took more than one person to pull me off of him. I felt empowered. I felt in charge.

The school principal got out his disciplinary board, the typical kind with holes in it. I'd been given hacks in nearly every one of my first six grades, but they didn't begin to compare to what I received at home. Nevertheless I suggested that the principal get permission from my father first. My dad had told me if I ever was hacked at school for fighting, he would do the same to whoever dished out the punishment. I don't believe that principal called my father, but he didn't touch me either. I suspect my father had a reputation.

Nobody picked on me anymore at Mari-Lynn grade school in Lyons that year. But I did poorly academically and was lucky I was not held back. I attribute my poor grades to a number of things: I was going through adolescence without anyone I could trust to talk to; my teacher simply was not very good; and, I suspect my mother's vigilance over attempting to change my teacher's vocabulary did not help my grades either, considering he graded on a curve. But I suspect a major contributing factor was Dennis leaving home. He had been caught stealing cigarettes and wine in Stayton. He also ran away once and made it all the way to Seattle, but a fifteen-year old getting off a greyhound bus with a sack of clothes looked suspicious to the depot security and he was sent back home. I even tried to run away the next day myself, but only made it a short distance off school property.

I discovered how much I enjoyed being alone. My paper route afforded me a couple hours a day to ride around town by myself. Listening to the pop music of the 70s gave me a sense of peace and comfort, especially when I took a long drag off the cigarette, blew the smoke out, and made smoke rings. No one understood me. I'm not sure how much of that was attributable to adolescence and what came from my perceived lack of love and acceptance at home.

I really liked a cute girl in my 7th grade class at school named Becky Foster and knew I wanted to do something with her besides just hold her hand, but I had no idea what it was. She hardly knew I existed, but I sensed she would understand me if she just knew me. One day I saw her with a cigarette in her mouth. I was so excited because I smoked too and we now had something in common! I ran up to Becky and said, "Hey, I smoke too," and showed her my pack of cigarettes. She started to laugh and showed me her candy cigarette. I was horribly embarrassed, but it didn't curb my infatuation.

When the school year ended my parents informed me that we were moving to Salem so Dad could go back to college. He wanted to become a pastor. I don't know why it made perfect sense to me back then, but as an adult it confounds me. But, I was happy to move. A fresh start. There was nothing and no friends in Lyons to hold onto.

The next year I got straight A's at Judson Junior High School in Salem, Oregon. Each school day started out down by the river just off school grounds where all the cool kids smoked, including me. I was so small that my P.E. teacher told me to go to the office on the first day because he thought I was in the wrong school. I was still picked on and my lunch was stolen frequently. I even walked into the creek one time on the command of a girl in the smokers group, rather than risk her throwing me in. The only possible explanation I can think of for my academic success was the lower academic standards they had compared to my previous small town schools.

Dad began his college studies and was deeply involved in his German and Psychology classes and Mom took a few classes as well. I was able to spend a tremendous amount of time away from my parents, and other than getting whipped a couple times for smoking, I cannot remember getting into any other trouble that year.

I had a few friends at the apartment complex where we lived, including a special woman friend in her early twenties. She would always let me visit and smoke. I was deeply infatuated with her though she did nothing to encourage any improper relationship. And, I did learn a little bit about sex that year. My mother came home from the store and when I was helping put away the groceries I discovered a box of sanitary napkins. I had absolutely no idea what they were. Mom simply took them from me and said, "Those are mine." The next morning I woke up to a *Gray's Anatomy* book on the living room couch opened to the page of a cross section of the female anatomy. This was the extent of my formal sex education. To further illustrate my lack of knowledge, there was the time I brought home from silk screening class a T-shirt that said "Dirty old men need loving too." This made perfect sense to me. Whether someone was clean or dirty should not be a reason deny love. When my parents questioned me about it I stood in front of them in total ignorance, shrugging my shoulders. They looked at each other, shook their heads and that was the end of it.

The college my parents were attending was in Monmouth about ten miles west of Salem. It was called Oregon College of Education but is now called Western Oregon State University. After just one year in Salem we moved to Monmouth to be closer to the college, and as usual, I was happy with the move. I really didn't care. My life in Monmouth as a freshman at Tallmadge Junior High was very much a continuation of the previous year in Salem. I enjoyed school. I was in the elite swing choir. I was in the advanced science class. I was not popular by any means but I was not picked on either. I still smoked and was able to keep that from my parents, which was not too difficult since Dad smoked in our house.

I tried out for a community musical put on by the college and landed a major part and we toured throughout Oregon where I debuted my soprano voice. For being so small I did well playing football, basketball, and softball in sandlot games, but my size kept me from playing in formal school competition. Wrestling of course was not prohibitive, so I joined the wrestling team at the ninety-eight pound weight class. My parents allowed me to participate as long as I could get home from practice and the matches without needing them to pick me up. I loved going to away games. It gave me a feeling of freedom, but I wasn't very good. I won two matches, tied two, and lost sixteen. I don't believe either of my parents attended any of my matches or Danny's football games.

My mother worked in Corvallis, a nearby town, as an administrative assistant while Dad took classes at college, worked full-time as a pipe fitter (instrumentation), and began teaching instrumentation at the Salem local union training school. He quickly discovered the teaching materials were seriously outdated and lacking, so he began creating a training course with both slides and tapes. I barely remember seeing my father on any day other than Sundays when we went to church or occasionally on a Saturday when he needed my help, but I didn't mind.

One day, toward the beginning of the school year, a couple of kids from my swing choir class came to my house to visit. I had never had anyone over before, and it was awkward. I didn't want them there, but I didn't know why. I'm sure they recognized the awkwardness as well and never returned. I did not have anyone from school come to my house again. Looking back, I somehow knew in my heart that my family was different, and I was embarrassed.

For the most part, ninth grade passed without incident. I had a few whippings, but Dad was most often having me write essays (or "write words" as we called it) as his punishment of choice. Soon it was summer when I would pick strawberries with my best friend David. David had long blond scraggly hair and there was not a single organized tooth in his mouth. He did not have the best home life as his mother had been married nine times. But she let us smoke in the house and I spent as much time as I could over there listening to record albums. My favorites were Elton John and the Eagles. It was the summer of 1974.

When strawberry season ended I picked beans. Every weekday morning I'd wake up at 5:00 a.m. and ride my bike four miles through Independence to the bean field. I figured out that if I left the bean fields a little early and took my time going home I could stop at a hamburger shop or hang out at the park in downtown Monmouth. I absolutely loved the feeling of going where I wanted and doing what I wanted without my parents knowing. I quickly became addicted to it this and began leaving work earlier and earlier. I could not get away with skipping work completely because I needed to come home with some proof that I worked. Also, I needed some change every day to buy cigarettes.

One evening my father asked me how many pounds I'd picked that day. It was about 100 or so (at four cents per pound, I should have had $4.00). He told me not to come home the next day until I'd picked a minimum of 200 pounds. That was crazy. How could I double my output in one day? But with my fear of consequences as a motivation I picked over 200 pounds the next day. When I told my father he said "Good. Tomorrow don't come home until you have picked at least 300." That would be impossible, I thought. But the previous day I realized I simply had not been working very hard. So

I went out the next day and came home with tickets totaling 316 pounds. Every day after that I averaged about 250 pounds. This was the first time I realized that we can always work harder than we think we can. Though very little of his discipline and rigidity taught me anything useful, I am thankful to my Dad for that lesson in the summer of 1974.

Overall, the 9th and 10th grade years for me were relatively non-eventful, but I still lead a dual life—one in front of my parents and teachers at school and another when I was by myself. For some reason my parents did not want me to have money. Actually, they didn't want me to have money to carry with me. I could have it in an envelope at home and could take some for a specific designated use, but I was not allowed to walk around with extra money in my pocket. In fact, one time my dad told me if I were to find a penny on the road I was required to bring it home and put it in the envelope.

During my high school years whenever I saw money unattended, I took it. I don't believe it was due to a sense of entitlement. It was more that having money that my parents didn't know about allowed me to claim some power. When I mowed a lawn I always understated the pay. I bought cigarettes of course (most small towns had no issue with selling cigarettes to minors in the early 1970's), and if I wanted a Bob's 19¢ hamburger and a coke, I bought it. Most of all, having money I controlled gave me a sense of value.

But things began to change in the summer of 1975. Danny went directly into the Marine Corp just a week after graduating from high school. That left me alone with my parents at meals. It was definitely awkward. What made it most difficult was that I simply did not like them. I didn't want to be around them. There was no closeness. There was no love, certainly on my part.

I had grown tired of picking strawberries and beans and got a job moving irrigation. It was tough, dirty work, but anything was better than picking fruits and vegetables. On the third day of work I took a bottle of Olympia beer from home and drank it during lunch. I thought it would be okay, but that afternoon I had to drive the truck back to the shop to get a pipe valve. On the way back misjudged the corner and did a complete Brodie in the middle of the street that sent up a plume of dust and dirt. My new job moving irrigation was over as quickly as it started.

Shortly after that I had the opportunity to smoke pot for the first time. I didn't get high, nor did I the next few times I smoked it. But I thought I did and that's what mattered. Smoking pot that first time removed any remaining filter that would have prevented me from trying anything new.

The Beginning of the End

When school started my junior year I was allowed to be the manager for the varsity football team. With this privilege came the invitation to my first party after a Friday night game. I sat in someone's house drinking a beer and smoking a joint and suddenly I forgot how long I had been sitting there. I could not stop smiling. I felt like I was floating. Finally I had gotten stoned. It felt awesome. I loved it, and it became my intent every day after that to be stoned as often as I could.

Two weeks later, after the next home game, I was again invited to the post game party at Mike Lindley's house. Mike had graduated the previous year, but his brother Ray was a year older than me. At around midnight I told Ray I needed to call my parents but I didn't want to go home. Ray suggested I tell them I was spending the night at his house. For most families, this would not have been a big deal. However, since I had never spent the night any anyone's house ever, this would become an issue.

Although I'd only had two beers and some weed, it was enough to allow me to think I could get away with ignoring my dad's command to return home. I gave him Ray's address and went back to the party. About a half hour later, Ray came up to me with concern written all over his face. His mother had called and said a man was banging on her door screaming "Where's my boy?!" Ray drove to his house and met my dad. He returned with the clear understanding that my dad was anything but typical. I knew I had to go home, but I was concerned about the level of Dad's anger. I had never directly disobeyed before. So I had Ray take me to the police station where I called my dad. Dad came in and seemed very reasonable in front of the sergeant on duty. I figured he was simply glad that I was safe and I had weathered the storm. Seconds after we walked out of the police station and headed toward the car I started to apologize. Before the third syllable my dad kicked me in my leg and told me to shut up.

The next evening, when we were eating dinner together, Dad said, "I want you to tell me who bought the beer for that party."

I said, "No."

My mother's fork stopped its way to her open mouth. For a moment, life just froze. Never, ever had I directly refused to obey a direct order. This was unheard of. Dad however appeared unfazed. "We'll go out into the garage after we eat."

The rest of dinner was finished in silence. I wasn't sure of his intentions until he pushed back his plate, looked at Mom and said, "Why don't you take a walk?"

Mom got up, cleared her plate, and went out the front door. Dad gestured with his head toward the back door leading to the garage. I stood, walked to it, turned the handle, and stepped out past the door. Without warning, the bottom of Dad's shoe planted solidly on my lower back and I went sprawling face first onto the concrete. For the next few minutes all I felt was the palm of Dad's hands on my face, head, and ears, and his shoes all over the rest of my body. I had challenged him.

But, this wasn't discipline; this was rage.

Dad had manipulated the world around him using fear and bullying so he would never face being challenged by another male. There is a good possibility I was the first. Even then it was not lost on me that none of the hits and blows actually hurt. Physically I felt nothing and I refused to give my father the information he was demanding. When he finally quit hitting me he told me that he already knew the name of the girl who brought the alcohol to the party and said it with smug self-satisfaction.

My real injuries came from his decision to go to the school and drop the names of football players and other classmates who attended the party. A lot of people got into trouble, and when I walked down the hall I heard the whispers and it got quiet whenever I walked by a group of classmates. I hadn't been very popular before the incident, and I was even less so afterward. The only person who didn't seem angry with me was Ray. He'd met Dad. He knew what I was dealing with at home.

Since I'd lost the position as manager of the football team I was expected to come home directly after school. My bedroom was in the attic, accessible from the garage and a side staircase, so I snuck out a lot. I was caught coming home one night when my dad had rigged up some pans in the rafters that fell and made a tremendous noise as I opened the garage door. I was hit hard upside my head that evening during our "discussion."

During another of our "conferences" he grabbed me around my throat with his left hand and slapped me hard with the other. I remember just looking at him, right in his eyes. I didn't smirk. I didn't smile. I didn't sneer. I just looked at him. He became enraged and screamed at me with his fist clenched and his index finger pointing at me, touching my nose. And I felt nothing. My father was unable to hurt me anymore. I'd withstood his best. Beatings, whippings, kicks, punches, slaps, rage. I was no longer afraid. After that, I did what I wanted. The fear of consequences vanished. The distance between my secret life and public life grew enormously. I continued to steal any cash that wasn't tied down and stole watches from the downtown drugstore. I got high nearly every day; yet, I still went home and feigned respect for my parents.

My father told me once that if he ever caught me smoking pot he would break both of my legs and I believed him. One day I came much too close to finding out if he would be true to his word. I came home from school and had a brief chit chat about my day with Mom. Ever since I was a child Mom would pretend to nibble on my ear. I endured it with mixed feelings as I got older. This time, however, Mom's face went from giggling to ultra-serious as she shoved her hand into my coat pocket. She pulled the pocket out, bent down and sniffed it. "You've been smoking again, haven't you?" she asked.

What she didn't know was that just an inch or two from her fingers, inside the lining of my coast, was a big bag of marijuana. I had purchased it that day from my brother who was staying in town at a hotel. I had a hole in my coat pocket and unbeknownst to me the bag found its way through the hole into the lining. I just froze in time and finally nodded, "Yes, yes, I've been smoking again." That was just way too close. I became brazen about smoking in the house. Again, with Dad smoking how could he know? I took a bath every evening, opened the bathroom window, and lit up. My attitude was, what would he do? Hit me? Ground me? I really didn't care.

Around this time, I got a job washing dishes at the Blue Garden Restaurant. On a weeknight in late April, 1976 with just a few months before finishing my junior year of high school I was at work. I passed by the cook's area and saw the cook's purse slightly open with a few dollars accessible at the top. As I had done so many times before that year, I looked around and, seeing nobody, reached down, grabbed the bills, and stuffed them into my pocket. My reconnaissance was less than perfect and the elderly woman cook caught me in the act.

It's difficult to look back and think, *What if? What if I wasn't caught? What if I had worked that Saturday as instructed by the manager instead of not showing up? What if I had apologized profusely?* Unfortunately none of us have the luxury of playing that game. At the time, I simply didn't care and had lost nearly all sense of respect for authority. I had survived. And I would survive again and again until the day I was offered the choice to live.

Four days later I was in the back of my parents Audi on my way to be dropped off at CSD in Dallas.

Chapter 4
ON MY OWN

The beat on the dance floor of the disco was unmistakable. "*Oooh . . . love to love you baby; Oooh . . . love to love you baby.*" The strobe light flashed continuously. The bodies writhed and glided against each other in sync with the music. I could have been dancing with someone, I could have been dancing alone. It didn't matter.

Just a bit earlier in the evening I handed three dollars over to the drug dealer who set up shop in one of the two restrooms and was handed a sugar cube dosed with a drop of LSD-25. I had taken "acid" once before but nothing happened and I assume I had been ripped off. This time it was the real thing.

Suddenly everything slowed down. The person in front of me morphed and I was looking at a pure white face with black eyes and candy apple red lips. I stopped dancing and looked around hoping to see a normal face. One by one, they all changed to something evil. I completely panicked and ran from the club, knocking over a few people on my way out the door.

The downtown disco was just a block off Broadway. When I got to the corner of Salmon and Broadway I felt helpless. I was unable to remind myself that I was tripping. I simply bought into whatever thoughts came into my head. None of them were good. I sat down on the sidewalk with my back pressed against the side of the concrete building. I called and waved to a pedestrian across the street. He came over and asked what I wanted. I said, "Help me, please."

He responded, "What?" He waited. I couldn't tell him. I couldn't even form a sentence to tell him what was wrong. After a few moments, he walked away shaking his head.

I had rented a room for a week at the Plaza Hotel just about four blocks north on Broadway. I could see the hotel's neon sign, but it looked so far away. My consciousness was overwhelmed with fear. I felt I was surrounded by evil. I began to walk toward the hotel, but the more I walked the farther away the sign became. I stopped and sat on the sidewalk a few times convinced that I had urinated on myself. Everyone's face turned into the evil white with black eyes and red lips. Those four blocks were a panicked, fear-ridden, tortured journey.

I did finally arrive at the hotel and found my way to my room. I used the phone in the room to call the number of a man who had come to visit us at MacLaren with a church group. When he answered I talked a mile a minute telling him I had taken some LSD and was on a bad trip. I'm not sure what he said, but what I heard was, "Just stay there. Calm down. Relax. Where are you? Stay there." The paranoia from taking the LSD got the better of me and I became convinced he was stalling me while he called the police.

I ran out of my room and took the stairwell to the lobby and froze when I saw an ambulance parked in front of the hotel with two paramedics pulling the gurney out the back doors. This was a really bad trip for my first time on LSD, and as if that weren't enough, I peaked right at that moment. I ran out of the hotel screaming, past the paramedics, across the street, and did not stop until I reached Burnside Street about five blocks away. In my mind I had escaped a night in the hospital or even jail. Perhaps from the running or simply the passage of time I began to come down and back to reality. I walked the streets of downtown Portland until the sun came up. When I returned to the Plaza Hotel the ambulance was gone. Perhaps it was just a coincidence . . . okay, it was a coincidence. But nothing could have convinced me that night that the ambulance wasn't there to take me away. I had been on my own for less than one week and the idea of being locked up again and losing my freedom simply scared the crap out of me.

Freedom was my lifeblood, so I did whatever I could to hang onto it. Freedom meant I could do whatever I wanted ... so I did. If I felt like hopping a Greyhound Bus to Seattle, I did. If I wanted to hitchhike to San Francisco, I did. But whatever I did or wherever I chose to go, it was not for the destination; it was for the (false) sense of purpose it gave me and a way to avoid responsibility. I would not stay anywhere for longer than a couple of weeks, but mostly just a few days. Sometimes, I would spend the nine dollars for a bus ticket between Portland and Seattle just so I could get in a good night's sleep. I did it so often that I got the timing down perfectly. I would fall asleep before leaving the bus depot and wake up just as the bus pulled into the destination.

There was another reason I stayed on the move. It refueled my sense of value and importance. Whenever I would come back to the streets of Seattle after being away for a week or two, my friends would receive me with signs I'd been missed. "How are you? Where have you been? Hey, let's get high!" I became addicted to their excitement over my return because it made me feel valued. But just a few days later the high would wear off and I was just another hustler on the street, just another kid trying to survive any way he could. When this happened, I'd hop a bus or stick my thumb out to go back to Portland where I'd receive the same warm greeting.

On one occasion, I had the pleasure of arriving in Seattle in style. A "customer" in Portland had given me the keys to his rental car, a brand new 1978 Olds Cutlass. I did not get the chance to thank him for it as I was quickly on my way, driving it north on I-5 to Seattle. I slept in the back seat for a few hours that night and by 8:00 the next morning I made a right turn off First Avenue right in front of the Donut Shop. A very attractive lady on the corner was peering in the window to see what stud would be driving such a fine car. I grinned back as the front right side of the car bumper slammed into the no parking sign. It was a good thing I was moving slowly, but I was more than embarrassed as the woman threw her head back and laughed at the child behind the wheel. Although, no one can say I didn't make an entrance that morning!

Later that day I parked the Cutlass on First Avenue just down the street from the Donut Shop. Just as daylight turned to dusk I walked by and saw that the car lights were turned on. I opened the driver's side door, leaned in and turned them off. Immediately a police car pulled in front of me and another pulled up behind me. A bullhorn sounded, "Get on the ground! Now!"

I relaxed my body, feigning submission, and stepped back out of the car, pretending I was going to get on my knees. Then I bolted. I believe I had the advantage because they never expected I was going to run. Within seconds I had a good lead as I ran toward Pike and crossed the street. After looking back and seeing no one I entered a business door and quickly ascended the stairs in front of me. It was a fitness club and the irony was not lost on me standing there, huffing, puffing, and taking deep breaths while trying to act completely normal. I asked a few questions of the receptionist, looked over some brochures and told them I'd think about it. I had stayed long enough that the street was clear when I left. I could not believe it; I'd gotten away.

Toward the spring of 1978 I saved enough money to get a studio apartment in Portland on the eastside at the Sergeant at Arms Apartments. Compared to the small hotel rooms without my own bathroom, this apartment was luxury.

During this same period I visited my parents who had moved to Tigard, a suburb west of Portland. They bought me a guitar—a Ventura 12-string—and I have no idea why, but I just loved it. I also ran into my old friend Dudley from MacLaren. One night Dudley, his friend, and I were walking around downtown when we came upon a kid about our age just walking by himself. We decided to mess with him a little. At first it was just verbal taunts. This was our turf, we told him. Suddenly Dudley's friend did a martial arts maneuver and kicked the kid directly in the face. I was emboldened by it and took my turn hitting and kicking him. He started to cry. It reminded me of Norman, the 4th grade boy I used to hit, and I suddenly felt very sad for him. I felt enormous guilt for his pain, for the lack of fairness. I was lying on my bed and taking a beating from my dad all over again.

But I kept all of this to myself and shared none of it with Dudley and his friend.

I kept my studio on the eastside for less than a month, but rarely stayed there. There was something lonely about the place in the evenings. It felt different from a hotel, which is temporary. It seemed natural to be staying there alone, but an apartment was permanent. Permanently alone. I didn't like it. Once I walked away from the studio I would not have anything remotely resembling a conventional life for many years to come.

The Seattle to Portland to Seattle thing was getting old. One or two weeks away from either city was no longer enough to give me the grand re-entrance that fed my ego. It was time to expand. I was drawn to the thought of visiting Los Angeles, San Francisco, or Hollywood. I had full confidence I could survive even though I didn't have a dime to my name. It was rare that I did not receive a handout when hitchhiking. And if Seattle and Portland had a downtown section for street kids, certainly larger cities would as well.

I packed my suitcase with clothes and my high school diploma and headed south on I-5 with my thumb out.

San Francisco

I instantly fell in love with San Francisco. On a bright and sunny Sunday morning that spring, I walked North on Polk Street from Market for the first time. Within minutes I found a group of street kids hanging out on the corner of Polk and Sutter. They were reserved, not the same as Portland or Seattle. That was okay with me. My agenda was to hustle up some money so I could get a hotel.

San Francisco is a gay city and I noticed immediately that I garnered a lot of attention. It felt really good. I would become addicted to it. I was never considered "good looking" in school, boys' homes, and shelter care, but in this world I was hot. A Shawn Cassidy type. I'd experienced this a little in Portland and Seattle, but never like this. Men wanted to talk to me, take me out to eat, and buy me drinks. They also wanted to have sex with me and I would . . . for a price.

San Francisco is a big city and there were many areas to stand and wait for a car to come by, stop, and negotiate. My favorite and most successful spot was standing on Powell and Geary across the street from Union Square. This was a high-priced area just down the street from the American Conservatory Theatre and the Saint Francis Hotel. Hundred-dollar tricks were not uncommon. This was more than enough for a few nights in a hotel, breakfast and lunch the next day, new clothes and, of course, a choice of premium drugs.

Less than a week after I arrived I took two Rorer 714 Quaaludes. If given the choice between uppers and downers, I would choose downers every time. I described the high as a "clean drunk." On this particular afternoon I was sitting in a restaurant on Polk Street having a plate of spaghetti and drinking a beer (another reason I loved San Francisco at age 18). The next thing I remember was lying on the floor looking up at paramedics. I found no particular interest in them at that time, so I resumed my sleep and woke up in the hospital in what I assume was the emergency room. I sat up, swung my feet off the hospital bed, stood up, and fell face forward on the floor. The orderlies helped me up, but I refused to stay. A police officer nearby told me, "Son, if we find you outside this room passed out on the floor, we will take you to jail."

I managed to find my way out of the emergency room, and I located an underground parking garage where I lay down between two cars and went to sleep. Sometime later I woke up and was able to walk to one of my favorite bars on Polk Street and Post. I walked in, my face and clothes dirty from road grit and grime. I said to the bartender, "Give me a greyhound, please."

As much as I loved San Francisco and would return many times over the next three years, it was time to go for now. I simply could not pull tricks for longer than a couple of weeks. The main reason was because I wasn't gay. I was performing homosexual acts for money, but I could compartmentalize. There was an important distinction between the act and who I was in reality. I could act gay, but I quickly realized that men who drove downtown looking to pay for sex were not looking for effeminate gay boys. They wanted boys who at least acted straight, even if they weren't. This, of course, was easy for me.

I was not without struggles in my sexual identity. There were many times I began to question my orientation, but not due to desire. Just due to confusion around my willingness to perform certain actions. A gay man I met at that very same bar on Polk and Post many years later explained it best for me. He said, "Having homosexual sex does not identify you as gay. Having homosexual sex with a same-sex partner who you love identifies you as gay."

I had street friends with sugar daddies who lavished money, jewelry, and gifts on them. Part of me wanted that, but I never could bring myself to do it. Accepting these tokens required relationships, something I couldn't fake.

There are many stories of the streets to share. Some are funny. Some are sad. Some reveal the danger associated with getting into a stranger's car. All the stories are interesting. But they simply do not add anything valuable to this book. It was a lustful, sinful, drug and alcohol-infested lifestyle that, with each transaction I made, cost me another increment of the innocence I had as a child. The longer I allowed my body to be used by another, the deeper the anger and the hotter the rage inside became.

Leaving the West Coast

My first trip to the East Coast took me through Las Vegas, Dallas, and New Orleans. When I was picked up hitchhiking and asked where I was going I simply said, "East." I robbed an elderly man my first night in Las Vegas at the Flamingo Hotel. He wasn't a trick; he was just drunk and lonely and I exploited the situation. When he passed out in his hotel room, I took all of his money except five dollars. This would become a habit—always leaving them with something. I also took his sport jacket, which was a little too big, and his alligator skin shoes.

With the $200 I got from him, I felt rich and rented a room for a week at a cheap hotel just off the strip. It had an outdoor pool and I thought my life had finally turned around. I could lie by the pool all day and drink at night without having to hustle. I even worked a day job for minimum wage helping with a renovation of the Sahara Hotel. Before the week was out, however, I lost what money I had left playing blackjack and I discovered that Las Vegas was a tough town for getting handouts. I could have been standing by a phone booth with my throat cut asking for a dime to call 9-1-1 and probably wouldn't get a single person to stop.

Again, it was time to leave. When I made the decision to leave, it became my mindset and there would be no deterrent. I lived on coffee change and the generosity of those who picked me up and dropped me off. I rarely waited on the highway for very long. The worst my situation ever got was when I'd have to find a 24-hour restaurant where I'd sleep on three chairs placed side by side in a back corner. More often than not a waitress would provide me with a free meal. If I were really lucky she would take me to her house, which sometimes belonged to her parents. Later she would take me back to the highway and send me on my way so I would not be around to reveal the event to her friends.

I finally ended up in Dallas, Texas. This was a city unlike any I'd been where I could tell a lady on the street corner that she was looking especially beautiful today and she would smile and respond with a "Thank you!" I had enough money to get a hotel room for a couple of days and I did some day labor—one day at a hospital laundry and another day washing dishes at a restaurant. I liked day labor because we got paid at the end of the day.

Liquor was relatively cheap, and the second night I was in Dallas I was drunk and stumbling by the Greyhound Bus Station. A Ford LTD idled in front, double parked and empty with the driver door open. It was an invitation I could not refuse. I jumped into the driver's seat, shut the door, and took off. Having a car to use was so much better than walking or taking the bus.

The next morning I found myself in the suburbs at a Days' Inn and Tasty World restaurant near the LBJ/I-635 freeway. I applied for a dishwashing job and was immediately hired since their dishwasher had quit that day. The best part was that I was able to negotiate a free room as part of my compensation. Since I no longer needed the car, I parked it in a gas station parking lot and dropped the keys in the men's room trash can.

A few days later an event occurred that I have never been able to explain. The details are as clear to me today as they were when it happened that summer evening at the Days Inn Hotel. Earlier in the day a seventeen-year-old girl—no, a goddess—walked into the restaurant with a tall, lanky boy and a burly truck driver. She was the most beautiful girl I'd ever seen. She was bronzed from the sun with brunette hair that cascaded over her shoulders. She wore a pair of jean shorts and a swimsuit top. I went about my business while eyeing her without shame. She caught me looking at her and smiled. I thought I was in love. At the end of my shift I found her alone by the pool. Never shy, I started a conversation and soon had her laughing. Later that evening I asked her if she wanted to get high and she said yes. The tall lanky kid was her boyfriend from Alabama and they had been picked up hitchhiking by the truck driver. The two of them had gone out drinking somewhere while Amanda hung out by the pool. This worked for me.

That evening Amanda and I smoked some bud and we just walked around and talked. I even held her hand. So far the night was going very well. We ended up back at their ground floor hotel room at dusk and decided to go in. I opened the door and walked in first. I was barefooted, and my third step in the doorway sunk into something wet and mushy. I flipped on the light. Lying down, passed out cold, was her boyfriend. He was in shorts with no shoes and no shirt. I was unlucky enough to have stepped in his vomit. We found out later he had taken several Valium along with a pint of Bacardi.

I asked Amanda to help and we each grabbed a wrist and drug his limp body out the door. I was angry not only over stepping in his vomit but because I had hoped to be making out with this lovely young lady by now. With her boyfriend out cold on the doormat, Amanda and I walked back into her room and shut the door. Just after I heard the click of the door latching mechanism, no more than four or five seconds later, a loud and violent crash deafened our ears, and I saw the kid's lifeless body fly through the window, soar over the bed, slam against the wall, and drop to the floor in a heap of human flesh. The quiet was broken by groans uttered from the kid's unconscious body. When I could finally move from the initial shock, I did a quick assessment and saw a silver dollar-sized chunk of flesh missing from his lower right back and called 9-1-1 from the room phone.

The ambulance came and hauled him away. The police asked questions—questions I could not answer. How did this happen? Did he get a running start and launch himself? Did someone throw him? The whole event left me shaking for the rest of the night. Of course, I was immediately evicted and not invited back to work. The truck driver rented another room and reluctantly allowed me to sleep on the floor. I was the last person he was hoping to have around, but the next morning Amanda talked him into taking both of us on down the road with him. He was going to New Orleans, which was just fine with me.

New Orleans

It was not Amanda's first time to New Orleans. She had "danced" at a number of establishments on and off Bourbon Street. She also was not new to the hustle. Amanda was popular on the street and drew a lot of attention, especially when she wore a halter top and a pair of daisy dukes. She was just a little more popular than I was comfortable with. The first night we made friends with a nice, young black man who invited us to spend the evening at his house. I got drunk and passed out. The next morning Amanda was in a hurry to leave. Apparently in the middle of the night our "friend" and host woke up my girlfriend, dragged her to his room, and raped her. The life I had chosen to live—choosing not to work but still needing to survive—was tough. We needed sleep and food. This would put me and others in risky situations. Sometimes I was the predator. Sometimes I was the prey.

But, I did enjoy the all the debauchery New Orleans had to offer. Regardless of whether or not I made money hustling or stealing, I seemed to have a bottle of Wild Turkey close by. For some reason the burning of rot gut whiskey going down my throat seemed to be reasonable punishment for the amount I drank. About a week after arriving in New Orleans I stumbled out of a bar on Bourbon Street just after midnight—the day of the week never matters in New Orleans—and I saw Amanda standing across the street laughing. Even in my drunken stupor I saw how beautiful she was. Her arm draped around another man, she clearly had found a companion for the evening. She suddenly stopped and our eyes met. Briefly. But she turned and walked away, arm in arm with her new friend.

Something snapped. There was not enough alcohol in my system even after a week-long binge to hold off the feeling of abandonment. I had felt that too many times before—each time my mother took a walk so she didn't have to hear a beating, when my parents drove away after dumping me off at Children's Services Division. And it was washing over me again.

I turned and faced the first store window I saw. My fist lashed out and the window disintegrated into tiny glass particles. I walked a few feet down the sidewalk and challenged another window. And another. The fifth or so window was a jewelry store window and it shattered with the immediate scream of the alarm system. I looked at my right wrist and the blood arching out, bathing the inside of the store, sidewalk, and gutter.

I had nearly cut my hand off, and I didn't feel a thing—just the ache of abandonment, of being alone.

The police arrived quickly and I swung at them with both my good arm and the bloody one. I was taken down forcefully to the gutter mixed with dirt, grime, and the fountain gushing from my wrist continued. With my long hair firmly in the grasp of one of the officers, he smashed my face into the pavement. I felt the grit in my teeth and gums. They held me there until the paramedics arrived and I lashed out at them as well. With my wrist bandaged enough to stop the bleeding I was transported to the hospital emergency room. At eighteen-years-old I was no different from the stereotypical skid row pain in the ass. After trying to get up and run a couple of times they finally handcuffed me to the gurney railing. In short order I was in surgery and received forty stitches both inside and outside of my wrist.

After a couple days in the hospital a police representative notified me that there would be no charges. Apparently there were enough witnesses to my face bashing that there was some concern I had a case against them. After our discussion I pulled out my IV, left the hospital, and went immediately back to Bourbon Street where I found a street guitar player. I played the left hand chording, he strummed with his right. Other than having a cast on my right arm, things were good and the music soothed my wounds. I no longer thought of Amanda and assumed she had found some other troubled soul who would soon be launched through a motel window or would be taking their sadness and anger out on store front windows. It was also time for me to move on, and Houston was my next stop.

It Was Just My Turn

I had plenty of reasons to be scared of the guy. He was a big black man with arms like tree trunks. He was bald and wearing a dirty tank top. We were in a darkly lit parking lot in downtown Houston at the tail end of the evening. But I wasn't afraid because I believed I was the dangerous one. If I needed money I hustled for it or simply took it. People needed to be scared of me, not the other way around.

Perhaps the first clue was in our introductory conversation.

"Hey, buddy, wanna buy some weed?"

"No, thank you," I responded.

"Then, do you have any to smoke?"

That didn't really make sense to me, but I actually had a couple of joints in my pocket, so we sat on a parking curb and I lit one up. He said his name was Chico. That was cool; he looked like a Chico. When he told me he had just gotten out of prison I still did not raise my guard. I had been in prison too. Not a big deal.

But, after we smoked the joint, stood up to leave, he suddenly grabbed me by the front of my shirt with his left hand and put a knife to my throat with his right hand. Only then did the alarm bells go off. He pushed me and made me walk backward until I was in an alley, about a yard distance between the two buildings. He gave the customary commands not to run or scream if I wanted to survive. I had no reason not to believe him. Then he told me the best possible outcome for me that evening was that I would be stabbed and someone might find me before I bled out and died.

I was quick to accept that this would be my fate as I did not see any alternative. In fact, I relaxed my body and he let go of my shirt. The knife stayed. I did my best to act natural, not showing any fear. Truthfully, being able to do that was a gift that helped me deal with what I was facing. He told me to empty my pockets, which I did. I had a couple of dollars; that was it. He went through my duffel bag and took a football jersey. After I gave him my watch, he said, "Now turn around and face away from me."

I thought of my mother. I always did when I thought I was going to die. I felt the same sadness for her then that I did when she drove away and left me at social services when I was sixteen. *She will miss me*, I thought.

I turned and waited. I had never been stabbed and had no idea what to expect. After about five seconds passed I thought maybe he'd just hit me in the head. A few more seconds passed and all of my five senses were at DEFCON 5. Then a few more seconds passed. I heard nothing; but, my sixth sense told me he was still there.

"Turn around."

My fear peaked again. I expected to turn and immediately be punched or stabbed. Maybe his conscience struck him and was too prideful to kill me from behind. I slowly turned in that narrow space between two buildings and faced him. He didn't say anything but just looked at me. I matched his stare and looked directly into his eyes. There was something familiar about those eyes. I'd seen it before. And suddenly I knew what it was.

I said, "Are you kidding? That's what you want?"

He nodded.

It wasn't money. It wasn't my watch or a sports shirt. It was me. Suddenly my experience hustling on the streets pulling tricks would be the experience that would save my life. I immediately became his friend. I told him that I liked him. I followed him first to a ghetto bar where I played pool. I got into a verbal confrontation with one of the black patrons and Chico's simple look at the gentleman made him back off, hands in the air in surrender.

He then took me to a studio apartment that was empty except for a filthy mattress on the floor. It reeked of feces and urine. And, it was there he raped me.

Afterward he walked with me to a 24-hour restaurant where he bought me a coffee and breakfast. It was if we were a couple of college buddies catching up, talking about older, better times. And then he left. I sat there for a few minutes and shed some tears. When I looked around I saw normal people, eating, talking, and laughing. They had no idea what I had just been through and, while I wanted to tell someone, what could they possibly do? I realized, it was just my turn. I wiped the tears off of my face, grabbed my duffel bag, and walked out of the restaurant. It was done and over. I had survived once again. Back to the highway.

I headed back to Dallas long enough to collect some money waiting for me at the Tasty World restaurant. That allowed me to catch a greyhound bus back to Portland, Oregon. *Damn*, I thought, *life is just tough out there*. I would just need to get a little bit tougher.

Dennis

Regardless of where my journeys had taken me or how much money I didn't have, my oldest brother Dennis would receive me with open arms. It was an odd, multi-faceted relationship. While I have tried to tell my story without inviting the joint experiences I had with my brothers into it, certain dynamics of our interaction help to explain some of the darkness in my soul.

When we were kids, playing football behind the big white house in Scio, there were times after Dennis would tackle me to the ground when he would get a look in his eye and give me an extra elbow in the ribs or a kick in shins. It was unnecessary for the game. It was an aggressive, mean outlet for him. This was contrary to his normal state of being. Dennis radiated insecurity and could be difficult to be around.

From a young age I felt I was his protector. He would flip off a truck load of college kids and I would be the one to stand between Dennis and them when they would turn around and come looking for a fight. I was always ready to get physical, but my ability to talk would usually diffuse the situation. This scenario played out frequently.

But we had a common bond that brought us close together—the physical and emotional abuse we suffered at the hands of our parents and the fact that we each were kicked out of our home at ages fifteen and sixteen, respectively. Dennis would often pick me up at Hawthorne Manor in Corvallis and I inevitably returned wasted. We always got high together. It was our thing.

At the end of the summer of 1978, Dennis and I connected again in downtown Seattle. He worked at Sambo's restaurant as a cook. Dennis always worked, and it was nearly always at a Sambo's or a Denny's. And he was good. He had a reputation as an excellent breakfast cook, but with a temper. Waitresses hated to bring food back to him or tell him he got the order wrong. Dennis had no filter when it came to venting his emotions. I watched him destroy more than one pay phone and saw him throw his fishing rod, reel, and tackle box into the middle of a river.

We stayed at various downtown hotels and really had a great time together for a while. Dennis was my greatest fan and loved to just sit and hear me play guitar. But, we never talked about how it was growing up. And, unfortunately, our reunions always ended badly. More often than not I would end up chasing him in order to beat the tar out of him because he stole from me or because we were drunk and I felt the need to punch him. As a result I would gather my belongings and leave town. When I came back a few months later, we were always glad to see each other and all previous conflict was forgotten until the next fight. This was how it went with our dysfunctional brotherly love.

A Potential Girlfriend

The following year around the beginning of May I met Marty. She came into the VIP's restaurant in downtown Salem to get some coffee and saw me sitting at the counter, my guitar close by, but I didn't even have to play a song. Evidently, just having a guitar and backpack was enough to attract her because we ended up at her place.

If she knew anything about me we never would have even made eye contact. I had been up and down the west coast from San Diego to Vancouver, British Columbia several times on a consistent rollercoaster of using drugs, alcohol, and people until I ran out of options and had to move on to the next victims. I continued to get bolder during robberies, fueled by the alcohol and narcotics. My conscience became lost, smothered, and drowned. Marty saw me as a young, good-looking guy who was simply doing his thing before having to settle down into a conventional lifestyle. My chameleon-like ability convinced her this was true—just a carefree kid in a carefree world.

A few days later we drove from Salem to Reno where her grandparents lived. It was easy for Marty to get work in "The Biggest Little City in the World" and I went along for the ride. We arrived late in the evening and I was invited to spend the night at her grandparents who had an organ in their living room. After playing a few songs on their organ out of the Lutheran hymnal and agreeing that perhaps the book of James was never meant to be in the Bible, they were ready for me to marry their granddaughter.

Marty's grandmother fixed up the guest room especially for me. Such a nice bed. Unfortunately, I never slept in it. I had intended to slip back in there before anyone else woke up, but did not wake up in time. After discovering me in bed with Marty, my debauchery in their Christian home wiped out the memories of me singing "Amazing Grace" and spewing scriptures, and my place setting at the breakfast table was removed.

I took a Greyhound bus to San Francisco but returned to Reno a week later. I wanted to try for a real relationship with Marty. I really liked her. She was so responsible and always worked. I stayed at the home of one of her family friends in Sparks, Nevada. Their dog never let me walk around un-escorted. If I even acted like I wanted to move off the couch, the dog would growl and bare its teeth. I got a job with a landscaping company and even worked for two or three days. In the end, I was simply too immature. I didn't want to work. I was extremely jealous of Marty and didn't understand why she would want any friends other than me, yet, at night I would walk around 4th Avenue, visiting casinos and bars, playing guitar for free drinks, and had no problem hooking up with girls and older women. I never connected with the fact that I was cheating on Marty while expecting her not to talk to any guy but me. I had two lives and I conned and manipulated to make sure the two would never meet. I think Marty was happy when I told her I needed to hit the road. She even drove me to the highway. I left with my backpack and guitar. Leaving was just getting too easy.

In the summer of 1979 I hitchhiked again to the East Coast and back. I traveled with the guitar around my neck and played at least twelve hours a day. I was getting pretty good. This time I stayed relatively unscathed, although one misunderstanding with a truck driver in Little Rock, Arkansas, nearly cost me my life. He picked me up at a Waffle House off I-30 and I had no idea he had consumed nearly a fifth of vodka and a handful of cross tops (speed). It was dark when we left and within an hour we were in a thunderstorm, the likes of which I had never seen in my life. Lightning seemed to be hitting on both sides of the truck followed by the immediate clap of thunder. I don't recall when I first noticed him looking at me. He just stared. Another pervert, I assumed since approximately one out of three men who picked me up were looking for sex. I was used to it. Finally, having had enough of his empty stare I asked, "Are you gay?"

He didn't answer, but he did reach into his console and pulled out a shiny Colt .45 handgun. It was not uncommon for truckers to have firearms, but this was the first time I'd had one pulled on me.

I asked, meekly, "Are you serious?"

He then asked me, "You think I am, huh?"

"Yes!" I answered.

His right arm straightened out toward me, the revolver lowering to the left side of my head. As the cool end of the barrel connected with my temple, I heard the Colt's hammer make the unmistakable sound of being cocked into a locked position. I was less than one pound of pressure away from taking my last breath. As always, I thought of my mother and how sad she would be when she learned of my fate.

For a reason I will never know, the truck driver asked me one more time, this time clarifying exactly what he wanted to know. He asked, "So, you think I'm gay, huh?"

I said quickly, making sure my head didn't move, "No, no! I meant I think you're serious!"

He played out the conversation in his head one more

time and, feeling that he got the answer he was looking for, un-cocked the revolver, put it back into his console, and drove me all the way to Dallas, Texas.

The Carnival

Other than a few weeks here and there I was on the road from somewhere, going to somewhere else. The pattern of indulging in the sin and darkness of the city's dirty sections played out again and again. Most of the time, the men who picked me up and got me drunk were not happy at the end of the night. If they were lucky, I simply walked out with their cash or valuables, daring them to stop me. A few times I erupted in violence and left them a bloody mess.

I joined the carnival and fell in love with it. I quickly became one of those greasy, grimy guys mothers warned their daughters about. But I was a good-looking kid and, along with the nightly alcohol and drugs, came daily opportunities to exploit the carnival's lustful lifestyle. I was setting up a ride one morning in Puyallup, Washington at the Western Washington Fair when I found myself sitting high off the ground thinking of my father. *If he could see me now*, I imagined, *maybe he'd approve.*

It was the last stop for Funtastic Shows in 1979, but Dennis and I joined the carnival together in May of 1980. Port Townsend, Port Angeles, Everett, Lummi Island—I thought I'd found my home. We got $5 or $10 per day draw. Alcohol, drugs, girls. And protection.

We stuck together and I learned that calling out "Hey, Rube!" would instantly bring together a bunch of dirty, tough carnies to deal with jealous boyfriends.

Unfortunately, my inability to smoke pot responsibly and leave it for after work became my demise. I was responsible for making sure an electric winch cable did not get tangled and caught when moving ride tubs (cars) from one end of the van to the other. I'd already screwed up once and Guy, the big boss man, told me that the next time it happened he'd wrap the cord around my nuts and neuter me. He'd hit me in the face once, something I perceived as love, so I believed him.

But I was high that last day on the Indian reservation in Lummi Island, and my negligence caused the cable to get caught again and it ripped out of the winch, sending sparks to the van floor. Guy didn't follow through with his threat of violence, but he didn't have to tell me I was fired. And I gave him a wide berth as I got my stuff from the empty Jenny van, picked up my final check from the office trailer, and left the grounds. Lingering after being fired would just subject me to unnecessary hostility. I was doing dumb things, but I wasn't stupid.

Chapter 5
MEETING JESUS

Sometime during August 1980, after joining a few other carnivals, I was hitchhiking northbound on I-5 just south of Eugene, Oregon. A car with four kids in their late teens, just about to enter the freeway, stopped on the onramp. They said they were only going north for another exit or two but were happy to get me a little farther up the road.

It became clear almost immediately that they were Christians and had no reservations about sharing their beliefs. But, the ride was short, maybe just a few miles so there wasn't time for them to get too deep into it. As I got out of their car they said, "Hey, it's Friday night and you could probably use a meal and a place to spend the night. Why don't you come with us, spend the weekend, and we'll take you back to the freeway on Monday?"

It's funny that in the past I would have had no issues with following criminals to an unknown location with just the prospect of getting high. But somehow the idea of hanging out with some Jesus people for even one night was way too scary for me. I said "Nah, but thanks. I gotta keep moving."

They said they understood and then drove away. I watched their taillights for a minute and thought, *Man, why didn't I go? I'm hungry and definitely need a shower.* Suddenly I was sorry I had said no.

And just as quickly as they had left, they returned. One of them, Scott Cardwell, rolled down his window and said, "We really think you're supposed to come with us."

I looked in the car and saw Laurie who was certainly easy on the eyes and Brett who looked like a gymnast or a wrestler. It turned out that both he and Scott were outstanding wrestlers for the small town of Lowell. They looked innocent enough. I figured if they got too pushy with that religious stuff I could just leave. I'd done it before. I got in their car and went with them to a large house in Springfield.

Having grown up in the church I knew of God. What little I knew about him convinced me he was pissed off at me. Even the minimalistic church life of going every Sunday and putting some money in the offering plate was not a part of my existence. I was angry with my pastor who I felt failed to protect me from my father's rage. I was angry with anyone who told me Jesus loved me. How could he love me? He doesn't even know me. I doubted he followed me around the streets of Portland and watched me sell my body for drugs. I was afraid to say I didn't believe, but knew that I strongly questioned the whole story of the Hebrews and plagues and a body of water splitting in two.

Everyone at the house was nice to me. No one preached. They had a piano that I played just to show off for Laurie. I took a shower and felt better. In fact, I strongly considered grabbing my backpack and heading out the door then, but it was already early evening and they were going out to Joey's Pizza. I wanted pizza.

It happened while eating my second slice. It could have been the corporate love in the room. It could have been God simply touching my shoulder. For sure though, it was completely unexpected. I felt sadness, joy, guilt, forgiveness, and acceptance all at the same time. Tears welled up in my eyes. I tried to stop it. I was eating pizza, and whatever was happening to me, my logical side told me that this was not the time or place.

But I couldn't hold back the tears and they began to flow freely as if the dam simply crumbled. I felt as though I had been gone on a long journey and I was coming home. Someone important was expecting me. Someone had been waiting for me.

I got up and quickly walked up to Ed, Laurie's father. I couldn't talk, but Ed looked at me and instantly knew.

He said, "Let's go." I was happy to. I was afraid someone would notice I was crying in a public place. He took me back to the house in silence. We walked to his bedroom and our knees hit the floor. For the next thirty minutes we prayed and read various verses. "For all have sinned and fall short of the glory of God." (Rom. 3:23) "Whoever believes and is baptized will be saved." (Mark 16:16) Ed talked about the fact that we are not our own—we belong to Him. A tremendous weight seemed to lift from my shoulders. The desire for alcohol, pot, and other drugs was gone. I experienced a sense of freedom I had never felt before. This was a very different experience from sitting in the church pew.

Just a few miles outside of Springfield, near Jasper and Fall Creek, there was a group of houses owned by members of Ed's church. Larry and Pam Poggemeyer were the first to buy property in this area and were followed by the Porters, Wards, and others. I was invited to live with Mike Ward and his wife and kids. Mike knew someone at a welding shop called Duncan Manufacturing and I was given a job. Mr. Duncan had an old 1963 station wagon and I purchased my first car for $200. I also learned how to weld. Similar to when I worked with the carnival, I thought if my dad could see me welding, he'd be proud of me. Once I got to take a large truck and deliver product and pick up materials in Portland. I assumed everyone who drove by me on the road was thinking, "Look at that guy driving that truck! Wow!"

After a few weeks I heard that Danny was on leave from the Marines and visiting my parents in Monmouth. It would be the first time for Dennis, Danny, and I to be together since 1972. Dennis told me he had been robbing people at rest areas off of I-5. I told him I walked with Jesus now and maybe he should think about doing the same. Dennis moved that day to Fall Creek to live with the Poggemeyers. For some reason I too moved in with Larry and Pam. Dennis got a job cooking at Denny's and things were good.

But I was getting restless. Now that I no longer did bad things I thought maybe I could go to work for my father. He owned Casmey Instrumentation Service. I felt that I was good enough now and he would accept me. My parents agreed to hire me and even helped me get setup in an apartment in Monmouth. I had an empty apartment with no furniture except a bed and no food. They gave me $50 cash to get started, but I spent more than half of that $50 on a hanging potted plant, but it died in days because it was meant to be outside. I chose the plant because I wanted so badly to feel domesticated. I wanted to feel as though I had never left home and all that I experienced was just a bad dream.

The first thing my father asked me to do when I showed up for work was to remove some screws from a Taylor Recorder. Within five minutes, both screws were stripped. I continued for another thirty minutes using every tool I could find, but to no avail. I failed at my first task. Dad walked over and saw that not only was I unsuccessful with my one assignment, but I had managed to make it worse. Without hesitation he picked up a Phillip's head screw driver, gave it a push and a twist and popped out the first screw with ease. He did the same to the second then set the instrument down, looked at me, and shook his head before walking away. I just absorbed the shame. I'd done it before.

I was incredibly lonely. And hungry. I had to eat somehow, but I could not ask my parents for an advance. It was so much easier on the streets of a big city. So many ways to make money. I remembered a family that lived across from my parents on Sacre Lane. The mother was a piano teacher, the father a college professor. I decided to visit them at 4:30 p.m. and asked to play their piano. At 5:00 she asked me if I wanted to stay for dinner. I did.

I was successful at this four or five more times until their teenage daughter Kristin brought it up as dinner conversation that I always seemed to want to play the piano around dinner time. That would be my last dinner with them.

One day, less than two weeks after moving to Monmouth I stopped by to visit my parents. Dad was still at work. I sat in the living room and talked to Mom for a while. When Dad walked in the door he just looked at me and walked away. I wasn't sure what

I had done, but he certainly wasn't happy to see me. After a few minutes he walked into the living room and said, "I just want to be here alone with your mother." I couldn't tell if he was embarrassed to say it or if he was embarrassed to think it. I walked out, hitched a ride to nearby Independence (Monmouth was a dry town) and bought a six-pack of beer. I didn't know how to feel hurt, but I was angry. It was the only time in two weeks I had visited my parents and I was immediately rejected.

I moved back to live with the Poggemeyers, but my attitude had changed. I began to see Christianity as nothing more than a set of rules—don't spend the night with a girl even if you don't have sex with her; don't wear your Budweiser shirt. Don't, Do, Don't. Larry and Mike sent me to a friend's house in Toutle, Washington where I worked security in the Red Zone at Mount St. Helens. But the one time I was actually needed to help locate a poacher I was stoned. They fired me.

Back in Oregon I met a girl, Tanya, who had an incredible singing voice. She and I traveled to Montana playing music at every bar and tavern we could find. I drank to get drunk every day. From that moment on I tried desperately to kill the truth of what happened at Joey's Pizza that Friday night. I drank, destroyed hotel rooms, and got into fights in Bozeman, Billings, Stanford, Lewistown, and Great Falls. I was not particularly nice to Tanya. I didn't love her, but I wasn't capable of loving anyone. We got a ride from a truck driver all the way to Phoenix, Arizona.

Shortly thereafter Tanya wanted to go back home to Albany, Oregon. I was fine with that. Unfortunately the guitar which was hers needed to stay with me. She could go. The guitar stayed, but I had to pry it from her fingers.

Leaving Jesus

While riding a small motorcycle in a Phoenix, Arizona parking lot on January 1, 1981, I was hit by a car. I landed on my face, putting a hole in my lip and breaking two teeth. This was a game changer. For three years, regardless of the circumstances, I could always rely on my looks to help me secure at least the fundamentals for survival. Now, not so much. My lips were five times their normal size, and scabbed. One of my front teeth was gone, the other broken in half. The four-inch bandage covering the hole just beneath my nose along with multiple scabs on my face was absolutely repulsive, even to me.

I had been working at a Denny's Restaurant and out of pure compassion one of the waitresses let me stay at her apartment. I suppose the waitress felt a little guilty since I purchased the motorcycle from her brother. She had a female roommate, a biker type who had made out with me a couple times prior to the accident. It took only a few days of me living there, staying loaded on Tylenol with Codeine and alcohol, before they asked me to leave. I said no.

Monday morning, January 5th, 1981 I pretended to be asleep as they tried to wake me up. They told me to be gone before they returned home. They knew I heard them. Soon after they left I began drinking. Heavily. All day. I went to my favorite bars and begged for free drinks. I suppose the bandages were good for something. In the late evening I returned, stumbling drunk to find a bag with my belongings on the porch. I tried the door handle, but it was locked.

Just like nearly five years earlier, I was kicked out. Unwanted. Rejected. Only this time I didn't blame them. I had nothing. I was nothing. In my mind, even Jesus wouldn't have me. I was worthless, just like my father used to tell me. He was right. I truly had nothing to lose.

I took a step back from the door and rammed it with my shoulder. It didn't give, but it splintered. The biker chick inside screamed at me to leave and I heard the unmistakable sound of rummaging in the kitchen knife drawer.

I stepped off the porch and looked around. On the ground by my feet was a two-foot piece of rebar. Close to that I saw a wooden two-by-two about as long as a baseball bat. I chose the baseball bat and walked back up the steps to address Ms. Biker who had opened the door and stepped out onto the porch, kitchen knife in hand. The wood club was in my right hand and resting on my shoulder like a batter waiting for the pitcher to finish drying his hands with the rosin bag. There were a couple of f-words thrown back and forth, but I suddenly felt very calm. It was the calm that came when I was about to act out with violence. The last thing she did was laugh, call me a pussy, and tell me I wouldn't do anything.

I took the bat off my shoulders and waited for the pitch to reach the plate. I had played a lot of softball growing up and I had a good swing. She really didn't believe I would do it, because she just stood there. She didn't duck or put up a hand in defense. When I swung for the fences it caught her square in the jaw. My hands followed through on the swing as I had been taught. She crumpled to the ground without a sound. She was out cold.

I ran. By the time the sirens interrupted the peaceful winter night I was blocks away. Within a couple of hours I had hitched a ride north on I-17 and was well out of reach. I called the restaurant a couple of days later and talked to the waitress. Her roommate had lived, but apparently I had shattered her jaw in numerous places.

I felt nothing. I wasn't happy about what I did, but I believed I was justified. It wasn't the first time I had been violent, but it was the first time for something other than to rob someone. This time was different. She represented every person in my life who had rejected me. She really did nothing wrong; it was just her misfortune to be in the wrong place at the wrong time.

The Crime

I robbed, stole, and inflicted terror all the way back to Seattle. I was not just sneaking around stealing when no one was looking. I liked the power and control I felt when I took from someone watching. My eyes dared them to stop me. I felt invincible. Nobody could tell me what to do. It was almost a distorted sense of nobility, and it would be my downfall.

I met Dick at a gay bar on 2nd Avenue and even with my face still a mess, after having a few drinks we agreed to an exchange of sex and money. One thing I remember about Dick was that he seemed to have hundreds of sweaters. They were all stacked up against the walls of his bedroom and hallway.

Dick worked in a record store and took a liking to me probably because I was a musician. And a young man. I tried to talk him into more exchanges where money was involved, but he was looking for a relationship. The last time I saw Dick he offered me a sweater and some Percocet pain killers. It kind of pissed me off. Of course, by this time, it didn't take much to get me there.

I was living with some heroin junkies at a flop house on Capitol Hill. Wednesday, February 18th, 1981 started out with me wanting to make some peanut butter crank. This was homemade meth cooked on a stovetop. The only thing I did not have was Benzedrex inhalers, the active ingredient. Each inhaler had a cotton cylinder which was used to manufacture the meth.

I walked to the nearest drug store, found the boxes in the cold medicine aisle and grabbed two of them in plain sight of the clerk staring at me from the cash register by the front door. He was staring right at me. I stared right back and my eyes never left his as I made my way toward him, the boxes of inhalers in plain view. My eyes dared him to stop me. I kind of hoped he would, as I was feeling that eerie calm I always had just before exploding in violence. I turned the corner at the end of the aisle, just six feet away from him, and walked out the door. He didn't follow.

I made the peanut butter crank, managing to do this without blowing up the apartment. There was Joe, his girlfriend, and Neil. Neil was a bad guy too. He was a junkie with a nine millimeter revolver. We smoked some pot, drank some wine, and mainlined some crank. A friend of Joe's had some window pane acid. It was a perfect high. I very nearly got high enough to forget about Jesus.

I began to think about Dick. He told me he took the cash box home every night from the music store. And I remembered that the last time I saw him he made me feel cheap with an offer of a sweater and pain killer.

I got Joe and Neil together. "Hey guys, wanna rob someone?"

That's all it took. Both of them were immediately on board. We waited until 11:00 p.m. and drove to Dick's house in North Seattle. I asked Neil if I could be the one to hold the gun on Dick. What he didn't know was that I planned to shoot him. I wanted to kill Dick. I needed to do it.

When we got to Dick's house, his car was gone. But Dick lived in the downstairs section of a duplex and had told me that two men lived above him on the second floor. I asked Joe and Neil if they minded if we robbed the men upstairs. I was determined. My friends had no other plans.

I went up the stairs on the outside leading to the second floor landing. Neil followed but would stayed out of sight until the door opened. It was now about midnight and starting to rain. I knocked and heard voices and movement inside. The door opened and a large, well-built man in boxers opened the door.

"Does Dick live here?" I asked.

"No, he lives downstairs."

"Oh. I'm supposed to meet him here. Would you mind if I waited inside?"

The man looked in my eyes and at that very moment he saw any remaining light fade and darkness take its place. He tried to shut the door. It was too late. Neil stepped up with the 9mm pointed directly at his face and said, "We'd really like to wait inside."

We made them strip and tied them up on the bed using torn bed sheets. Neil voiced his concern about "the big guy" and made sure his knots were extra firm. We took our time going through the house, removing anything of value and transferring it to the car. I felt extremely powerful. Neil allowed me to handle the 9mm. I put the business end into the ear of one of the men and asked him if he were scared. At that time, the I-5 killer was making the news, and since this house was so close to this freeway, I implied that perhaps I was in fact the I-5 killer.

I never pulled the trigger as I wasn't angry with them. In fact, I felt nothing for them. I'm convinced, however, that I would have shot and killed Dick Woodruff if he were there. I may have left Jesus then, but I'm quite convinced He never left me.

We left them naked and bound on the bed. I found out some time afterward they packed up a few weeks later and moved to San Francisco where they felt safer. Little did they know, I would have done the same there or anywhere else.

Two days later I packed a suitcase with a few trinkets stolen from the home invasion and hopped a bus to Salem, Oregon. I sold a camera for one hundred dollars, bought some LSD, and paid for one night in a hotel room. I was back where it all started. I had hitchhiked cross country twice and traveled up and down the west coast too many times to remember. Sometimes I'd been the perpetrator and other times I'd been the victim. My survival usually meant someone's loss. I had met Jesus and then said goodbye.

I was now back in the city where I'd spent my youth and attended church. It was also where I spent time in

Shelter care and tried to make it on my own while living at the YMCA and working at the Tahiti Restaurant. Just a few blocks away from the hotel was the bridge where I jumped out of Roger Mattson's car and ran to meet my girlfriend just one last time before going to MacLaren. Only fifteen miles south was the old white house in the country where my father would take the stairs down into the basement, start up the table saw, and cut off a chunk of plywood to be an instrument of punishment. And just fifteen miles west was the Social Services building where I watched the red tail lights of my father's car as he and mom drove out of the parking lot, leaving me and their parenting responsibilities behind.

In 80s there were some hotels that allowed me to pay for one night and stay another night or two with the expectation to pay before leaving. On Sunday, February 22nd I discovered the hotel I was staying at was not such a hotel. When I returned at around six in the evening I found that my guitar and suitcase had been confiscated and were in the possession of the hotel manager. All of my money was gone. There was nothing else of value to sell. I had one option: find a billy club, and select a victim.

It was starting to lightly rain. The streets were well lit, but there were storefronts and alleys with enough darkness to cover my deeds. I stopped on a street corner and waited for the walk sign.

It happened without warning. It came without expectation. Some people might call it a vision, others a faith picture. It would be easy to blame it on the drugs. It could have been God. I'll never really know, but I saw it with perfect clarity. I saw a five-year-old boy in his pajamas on the front porch of a big white house in the country. The porch faced east, and the morning sun lit up the porch like a spotlight on a theatre stage. And the boy . . . he wore his innocence like a blanket—his life not yet tainted with fear, pain, horrible acts, or unspeakable depravation. The contrast between the boy's undefiled innocence and the sins of the man on the street corner was powerfully overwhelming. I just asked myself, *What happened? What happened to that little five-year-old that could turn him into this lost man with a billy club in his coat?*

I started to cry. I sobbed. I said out loud for anyone to hear, "God, if you're real, you gotta do something." That, perhaps, was my first real prayer. It was simple and honest. On that night (although I didn't know it then) I received the most precious gift from God. He gave me desperation—nothing like the times I'd felt so desperate for a meal or a place to sleep that I sacrificed my soul. This was desperation for change. It was a moment of clarity, however brief. And I took advantage of it.

I walked to Sambo's on Commercial Street. We used to go there often after church. Without a penny in my pocket I ordered a turkey dinner and ate all of it. I called my father collect from a pay phone in the restaurant.

Our conversation was brief, but I told him I'd lost feelings for everyone and lost feelings for myself. He responded that that was a bad place to be. I said, "Yeah."

The manager was surprised when I told him I couldn't pay for my dinner and even more surprised when I asked him to call the police. I explained I was turning myself in for a robbery in Seattle. The two policemen took just a few minutes to arrive since the police station was right across the street. After giving the officers a few facts about the robbery, they made some calls to check out my story. It didn't take long to validate my statement and I was in handcuffs once again. They asked the manager if he wanted to press charges for not paying the bill. He reached across the table and took the check in his hand. "No," he said, "I got this one." I smiled and thanked him. I knew going in he would have sympathy for me.

Chapter 6
PRISON

This book is not about prison. It's not about all of the things that supposed tough guys do to weak guys in the showers. Even if I provided all of the details of my five-year experience, it still wouldn't compare to the license taken by TV and movie producers. True prison life is much more subtle. It's about fear. The results of being afraid and the unwanted activities are secondary. By the time these events occur, fear has immobilized the victim much like how a spider traps its prey in a web and bites it, injecting fluid that causes paralysis. The spider can then do as it wishes.

For the most part I knew how to do time. I spent the first 3 ½ months locked up in the old King County Jail. There are fights in jail nearly every day, mostly due to arguments over the phone or TV. It is mostly a place of transition and everyone is on edge. Was I afraid? If I were to get into a physical confrontation I would be. I always knew that there was the outside possibility that would happen. However I had confidence in my ability to talk my way out of anything. And I never used the phone and could not care less about what was on TV. The thing I had to worry about was whether I could keep my mouth shut when necessary. In jail I could. Later on in prison, unfortunately, I would not be so disciplined.

My main hurdle in jail and prison was the same as I experienced in high school, boys homes, JDH, and MacLaren. I didn't fit in. I simply didn't fit the part of a convict. I still remember an older con saying to me, "Man, what are you doing? You really don't belong here. You should be in college." I went back in my mind to high school where I didn't fit in with the stoners because I received above-average grades. I didn't fit in with the smart kids because I smoked cigarettes and pot. I didn't fit in at MacLaren because even the staff didn't understand my vocabulary, and now apparently I wasn't going to fit in at prison.

Main population in the old King County jail was brutal. Luckily, I was able to spend most of the 3 ½ months in the Trustee tank (tank=physical block of inmates) because the weapon addendum to my charge was not added until June 3rd when I plead guilty and had the sentencing hearing. (A home invasion robbery was classified as 1st Degree Burglary when armed with a deadly weapon). I worked in the bakery and the library and had a much safer existence than those in the main population. I had some issues but managed to stay out of fights. After sentencing I was removed from the Trustee tank and was put back into the main population for one week, and managed to stay below the radar.

On June 10, 1981, one week after sentencing, I was awakened early in the morning. The guard shackled my feet and hands to a chain around my waste. I was chained to inmates on my right and left and I was transported to the prison, Washington Corrections Center in Shelton, Washington. Everyone sentenced to prison in Washington State first went to the Receiving units at Shelton before they were transported to their final destination.

My introduction to prison did not start well. After just a few days, the inmates in all three R-unit cafeterias refused to go back to their cells. In addition, many of those still in their cells, including me, set fire to their mattresses and rattled their cell door bars. Shaking cell door bars along with a few hundred men screaming obscenities, was deafening.

This would be my first exposure to the "goon squad." The goon squad consisted of large angry correction officers who had been called away from their comfortable homes and families during the middle of dinner to dress up in riot gear to quell a mini riot. It was unwanted overtime.

Leading the charge was the superintendent, Harvey. Harvey had been shot in the face by a fellow guard in Walla Walla who caught Harvey in bed with his wife. It was Harvey who stood in front of my cell, A1. With ten guards behind him outfitted with riot gear, shields, and batons, he taunted, "Hink is hunny now? Hink is hunny now!?" Translation: "Think you're funny now? Think you're funny now!?" It was difficult to understand Harvey considering much of his jaw was missing.

In truth, I wasn't scared, but I was humbled. When the door racked I turned around with my hands above my head facing away from the CO. On his command I removed all of my clothing. While being prodded with a baton on my backside, I walked backward out of my cell and stood while every single item in my cell was removed. Everything. That night we were given the choice of sleeping naked on a metal slab or the concrete floor. We received sack lunches the next day and were given a blanket that night. The next day, more sack lunches and a toothbrush. Our personal property was reinstated an article at a time over a seven-day period.

I had to attend a hearing with Harvey and other staff who had the authority to make my life more miserable than it already was. I used the defense that my life would be in danger if I didn't go with the flow. I was questioned about the ring leader although I had no idea who it was. After ten minutes of questions, Harvey dealt my punishment: "erty ays oss a ood ime!"

Translation: Thirty days loss of good time. With an eight-year sentence, that actually hurt. And I hate to say it, but even now I enjoy making fun of Superintendent Harvey.

The R-units were extremely overcrowded and unable to handle the quantity of inmates being sent to prison in the state of Washington in 1981. This was an opportunity for small city jails to rent out space to the state and make some extra cash. I was sent to one such jail in Port Angeles, Washington. I spent six weeks in the Port Angeles jail before returning to Shelton; but this time I was on the main population side in Spruce Hall. Spruce Hall was another temporary stay while they determined in which of the three other buildings I would land. We were able to mingle with the main population from Cedar, Pine, and Evergreen halls, but only during mainline (chow). I made some friends from Evergreen Hall—a couple of guitar players—and I was hoping to be assigned there.

I was assigned to Evergreen and finally began to settle down and begin serving my time. At that time, inmates could work toward an Associates degree, so I signed up for some college courses. I even spent a little time around the weight pile though I had no idea what I was doing. I got to spend time every day with Joe, a fantastic guitar player and singer. For a few months everything was going well, considering where I was. But my inability to keep my mouth shut changed all that.

We had an old con names Snake in Evergreen Hall who did a bad dope deal with a couple of Latino guys. They took exception and caught him in an uncontrolled area and split Snake's head open with a pipe. I watched while Snake's buddy sewed up his head with fine fishing line. Even though Snake was originally in the wrong, a bunch of guys made a plan to attack the Latinos in the yard the next morning. I had no reason or business getting involved. It had nothing to do with me. But I felt the opportunity to contribute would further my goal of being in the inner circle. Looking back, as intelligent as I seemed to be academically, I really had no sense at all.

Nearly all of the Latinos were in Pine Hall. About fifteen of us created typical prison weapons made out of toothbrushes and razors. I had a pipe I had used before. When the doors opened to release us from our hall to walk to the kitchen, we went out into the yard and waited for Pine Hall's doors to open. My adrenaline was pumping. I felt tough, but only because I was one of fifteen. Just being there raised my status considerably.

We waited. And waited. But the doors never opened. They never came out. We assumed they had chickened out and eventually dispersed.

Later that evening after dinner I was talking to another inmate about the event. I was bragging how these guys were pussies and they didn't want any part of us. Behind me I heard a voice, "Hey! Puto!"

I turned around. It was Juan Gonzales, the unofficial

leader of the Latino group. He had heard me running my mouth, and he wasn't pleased.

"The guards knew you guys were out there. They kept the door locked and refused to let us out. But now, vato, it's you and me. We're gonna go at it. Monday during class break." And with that he turned and walked away.

I was really scared. On Monday I had difficulty concentrating on my college class with Juan in the classroom. I felt his eyes on me. When the time came for our break I walked out the door and faced him. I also had about five guys from my hall behind me who were ready and willing to jump in and keep it a fair fight. But, everyone knows in prison there is no such thing as a fair fight.

I took my stance and Juan immediately rushed me and tried kicking me. I stepped aside, caught his foot, and pulled it causing him to fall to the ground flat on his back. Immediately my friends started yelling, "Kick him, kick him! Jump on him!" But I had a little problem. I wasn't angry with Juan. I defended myself, but did not have it in me to finish him off.

Juan got up and came at me. Again he used his feet to kick at me, and again I caught one of them and took him down. My friends were screaming for me to tear him up. I couldn't do it. And then the guards came around the corner. We scattered to various corners of the yard. I was under the mistaken impression it was over. As far as I was concerned, we'd fought and there was no winner.

Unfortunately, Juan had to save face. His position as leader meant he couldn't let it go; he had to win. I was told I had to fight him again.

The next day we went into the flats (restroom) squared up and fought again. Juan simply did not know how to fight. Frankly I wasn't much better, but this time Juan's cousin tossed him a walking cane that he managed to strike me on my shoulder, barely missing my head. I wrapped Juan in a headlock and got a couple punches into his face. And again, the guards came and broke it up.

That evening, Juan met me when I was leaving the food galley after dinner. I was alone and he had his cousin with him. His cousin reached in his pocket and pulled out his hand, which was wrapped around the unmistakable flash of a steel blade. He handed the knife to Juan who took a step toward me. I took about five steps backward very quickly. After another step from Juan, I turned around and walked away. I should say, I walked away swiftly, with a sense of urgency. And finally, that was it. Juan felt vindicated and he saved face in front of his peers. Just over a year later he and I faced each other in another prison. But this time we both worked together in the GED learning center. In fact, he taught me his job keeping school attendance, duplicating learning tapes, and other tasks. You could say we became friends. We didn't make the rules in prison. But we had to abide by them, and hoped to survive in the process.

The Bottom

Survival is dependent on finding someone to establish the upper hand, gaining leverage, or having something of value to offer. I decided my best chance to gain status was to deal drugs. This was not one of the better decisions I have ever made. This is how the deal was supposed to go down: My brother, Dennis, would wrap up an ounce of pot in three "balloons"—moistened marijuana wrapped tightly using electricians tape and shoved into a balloon—which would be handed to me during a visit. I would take the three balloons along with some Vaseline, walk to the bathroom and "keester" the pot. "Keestering" is a little more delicate way of describing where the balloons would be concealed on my person. I, in turn, would hand my brother $200 of "white money." White money or cash is considered contraband in prison. Its value is inflated exponentially simply due to supply and demand.

Keeping a secret such as this is extremely difficult. A few weeks before visiting day everyone wanted to be my friend. They gave me coffee or even smoked a joint with me a few times. By the time the big day came I forgot nearly everyone to whom I'd made promises. They, of course, remembered them well with inflated interest.

The day came. But it was not during normal visiting hours because they had come from so far away (Oregon), so it was considered a "special visit." And there were complications. We sat at a table in the middle of the visiting room under the continual watchful eye of a guard. He sat there reading a book, but glanced up often. I sat and talked with my two brothers for about ten minutes and asked the guard to use the flats. I wanted to do a dry run. The guard came into the visiting room and followed me to the restroom. I opened the door and he walked in behind me, watched, and waited until I finished relieving myself and washed my hands. This was going to be a problem.

As I sat and talked I came up with the proverbial plan "B." The water fountain was just out of the guard's vision. He let me get a drink without following me, but I would have maybe ten seconds to do the deed. I sat at the table facing the guard and Dennis was to my right. I nodded slightly and he reached down the front of his pants with his left hand, pulled out a sandwich bag with the three balloons, each about the size of a quarter in diameter. I took the bag and was able to put it down the front of my pants since Danny was sitting between the guard and me. I still remember being incredibly embarrassed in front of Danny, but I never for one second considered the consequences to either of my brothers if I were caught. Dennis made the decision to smuggle drugs into a state prison and was responsible for his own choices, but Danny was at Annapolis Naval Academy at the time, due to graduate in a few months, and he had a lot to lose.

I asked the guard for permission to get another drink, to which he just nodded and went back to his book. I got up and walked over to the fountain. There, in front of Danny and Dennis, I quickly pulled my jeans down and essentially raped myself with three six-inch-long, quarter-inch-thick balloons. The pain was nearly unbearable. The fear of getting caught was very real. I pulled up my pants, buttoned them, and walked back to my chair. I looked at Danny and muttered, "I'm sorry." He just looked down at the table. I quickly sneaked Dennis the cash and immediately stood up. "Guys, I gotta go."

After they left I had one more hurdle. After any visit we were always strip searched. I doubt any of us ever got used to it—especially the last part, where we bent over, spread our cheeks, and coughed. I'd heard stories of a piece of balloon sticking out where the guard would reach over, grab it, and pull. I was very concerned that this could be a possibility since the insertion was completed in just over ten seconds.

I had nothing to worry about. At least from the guards. But when I got back to the hall, the inmates were hanging around my cell like vultures. There was literally a line starting at my door and going down the hall. But I had the goods; I was the man of the hour. And after finishing the fun job of extraction and preparation, I learned I had smuggled in the best quality marijuana in a long time. Dennis had come through for me.

The most important lesson from all of this: don't deal drugs in prison unless you are tough enough to do so. Unfortunately, I wasn't, and nearly all of that incredible weed was taken from me. I did manage to get most everyone paid off, and those I stiffed were below me in the pecking order. Luckily the message went out that I had finessed a fat distribution deal, otherwise my reputation as a convict would have fallen to just below Chester the Molester.

A short time later I was approached by Randy Brady, the president of the weight lifting club. Randy was from the suburbs and I don't know why he was in prison. He had heard of my smuggling operation (by now the story had grown to the point that I had brought in a few pounds several times). He said his people would send my brother $100 in advance and all I needed to bring him was a quarter ounce of marijuana. With that $100 I could easily acquire two ounces. Of course, this time I would not tell anyone. It would be a secret. A secret only Randy and I would know . . . and maybe a couple of others.

On the day Dennis was to be visiting, Randy and I waited for my name to be called. Randy, myself, and about sixty others. Some people just can't keep a secret. After an hour passed I began to be concerned.

I wondered if he was searched on the way in. Maybe he was in jail. After the final minute of visiting hours ticked off the clock I got on the phone and called his house hoping to connect with Becky, his wife. Dennis live in Eugene, nearly three hours away, so, when he answered the phone I was stunned. When I asked why he was there and not in Shelton he said he couldn't get a ride. I told him there were about sixty-one other families that would have gladly assisted with the trip. Dennis apologized and promised to be up in two weeks.

The scenario played out again. But, this time, when visiting day arrived, I had probably doubled my debt. I had no discipline. I lived in the moment, so if I wanted coffee or cigarettes they were easily obtainable with the promise of a joint. In truth, I had probably overpromised based on the amount of pot I expected to come in. But now my moment was about to happen. It was all arranged and Randy was set to help me.

And once again, visiting hours passed as, one by one, all of my debtors shuffled back to their cells. When I called, Dennis answered the phone and I knew I had a problem. He hesitated, then spoke in a small voice. I could picture his head down. I'd seen it before.

"Dwaine, I don't have any pot and I don't have any money. I drank it. I'm sorry."

I exploded on the phone. I was enraged. And, knowing Dennis, although I was locked up and he was a three-hour drive away, he had probably locked all the doors by now and loaded his shotgun. His fear from this action would not leave him for many years. Yet, I was the one who was helpless. I begged and pleaded for him to send the money back or borrow money and buy some weed and bring it up as promised, but it's difficult to reason with an alcoholic. At the end of the call I had nothing but fear, dread, and utter frustration.

In prison I learned what it was like to be truly afraid. Randy was nice, at first. He understood that things happen, and he gave me some time. I also managed to keep the other sixty guys at bay for a couple weeks. But every day the noose tightened a little more. Every day someone would suggest their patience was thinning. Reputation is everything in prison. Guys from whom I'd borrowed had pressure on them from their friends to collect or they'd look like I'd beaten them. It's just the way it was and I understood how the game was played. For the first time in all of my incarceration I was facing the risk of being seriously hurt. It would be violent and brutal with nothing held back. There would be no pity. No sympathy. There could be quiet empathy. But I was stuck on the tracks and a train was coming.

My options were few. Why couldn't I have chosen an "average" convict? I could have fought my way out of my situation with an average guy. I knew how to fight dirty. I'd done it before. But I chose to do business with a supremely fit weightlifter. And Randy would come with his friends. Suddenly the idea of fighting Juan Garcia seemed trivial. I would have to sneak up behind

Randy when he was alone and kill him with a pipe. That thought invoked a new feeling that I had never felt before. This was a decision point for me. The proverbial fork in the road. If I solved my problem in this fashion I knew I could never go back. Violence would be my life. I would end up like Snake, sitting in a cell having a gash in my head stitched up with fishing line.

I could check myself into protective custody, which would provide temporary relief, but even PC inmates could be reached. Once you went into protective custody in any prison, it was very difficult to ever successfully live in main population again. I had a minimum of five years and only a year had gone by. Four years in PC—I couldn't do that either.

There was a third option that I suspect very few guys would think of. If I pretended to escape I would most certainly go to the "hole" (segregation). I might even be transferred to another institution. I would get more time on my sentence, maybe a year. But I was willing to pay that price. I was not willing to face the alternative of being beaten nearly to death by prison convicts.

While walking back to Evergreen Hall after dinner on a Friday evening, Randy Brady came along side me and said my time had run out. He told me he was receiving too much pressure from others and he had no choice at this point. He nicely told me that my brother had until the end of the weekend to repay "his people."

I never made it back to Evergreen. Instead of walking through the front doors I slipped past them to the west side, fell to the ground and didn't move. The sun was down, and at that moment, I was totally and completely alone. The decision had been made. As each moment brought more darkness I would slither on my belly farther and farther away from Evergreen. I had no idea what would happen when they found me missing. Would there be sirens? Dogs? Spotlights?

Finally I saw the double fence topped with razor wire. About thirty feet on the other side a security jeep faced the fence and me. I crawled closer. I was sure he saw me. I began to crawl on my knees. After a few minutes of complete silence, I stood up. The fence was less than twenty feet away. I was directly in front of the jeep. Had he called security? Were the dogs on their way?

Nothing. Silence. I yelled, "Hey!" and waved my arms. "I'm right here! Hey!"

Not a sound. I learned later the guard was sound asleep and never saw me. It would be his last day as a corrections officer.

At this point it was comical. I wasn't sure which way to go to find the Administration building so I started walking west. The building I entered was the corrections officers break area. When I walked into the room that most likely had never even seen an inmate before their jaws dropped and they seemed frozen in time. I told them I tried to escape and explained what happened (or didn't happen) with the security jeep at the fence. They cuffed me and took me to the hole. The next day I told the captain I'd had a drug deal go bad but I didn't want to check into PC. I'd rather sit in the hole and save whatever reputation I had left. And that's what I did. I spent six months of 1982 in the hole.

The Hole

It's difficult to determine exactly when and where I hit bottom. Maybe there were many bottoms. But if the spring and summer of 1982 were considered to be among them, then this bottom would stand alone.

Administrative Segregation (the hole or ad seg) took up two tiers of the WCC receiving units. The cells were not cement fortresses behind steel doors without windows like you see in "Shawshank Redemption." We were confined to a small 5' x 8' cell. The bed was a single metal slat coming out of the wall with a mattress. It had a stone sink and a metal toilet. There were bars, not doors, and we were allowed a toothbrush, soap, and state-issued cigarette tobacco. We spent twenty-four hours per day in the cell except for showers every other day, and occasionally we would spend an hour in the breezeway where we could walk. Or pace.

To be clear it was not the cell size, lack of personal items, and restricted movement that caused the most discomfort. It was the often occurring events of individual degradation that did the most damage to my psyche. Very few people in my life knew I was doing time in prison. Virtually no one other than the guards who turned the key knew I was sitting in a single cell for months on end. The days passed by slowly. The nights were often even longer. But within this world of monotony, silence, and living from one breath to the other there were screams. And blood. And insanity.

I adjusted at first, just as I always did. I became an entrepreneur. Some of the men in the R-units who were on their way to Walla Walla (Washington State Penitentiary) served our food and would sneak me paper, pencils, bread, butter, meat, and cheese. With a Bunsen burner fabricated from toilet paper I made grilled sandwiches on my metal bunk and sold them for cigarettes and coffee. I also acquired extra mattresses, blankets, deodorant, and shampoo.

One day a young gay kid, maybe eighteen years old, came into segregation. Actually, it's entirely likely he wasn't gay but just acted the part and had sex with men as a means of self-preservation, as was the case with many men in prison.

This particular kid, Todd, had an attitude problem and was always fighting with guards. One night, Bear, a large burly guard, was making his rounds and when passing in front of Todd's cell he received a cup full of urine in his face. Todd had about twenty-four hours to revel in the memory of his action. He bragged about it during the day and continued to yell and scream obscenities to all the correction officers. He was having a really good time in the hole. Until the next night.

Around midnight, Todd's cell was unlocked and two hardcore convicts on their way to Walla Walla entered Todd's 5 x 8 home. I heard loud verbal commands followed by shouts of cussing and resistance. Then came slaps and the thud of a body slamming against cell walls, a momentary silence, and then an ear-piercing shriek followed by more screams. After a minute or so the screams turned to crying and then whimpers. Finally, it just sounded like animals grunting in the forest, and then merciful silence. I held my hands to my ears, but my attempts to block out the sounds were as futile as Todd's objections. I heard Todd's door rack shut. Bear resumed his walk up the tier and finished doing his midnight count. Todd would not bother him again.

Then there was Don, just a couple cells down from me. Don came across as a very intelligent guy. He would share stories of his youth, and he and I would often talk into the night. Don had an evil man inside of him, though, that made me look like a choir boy. Don had a disturbing ability to target sad men and talk them into slashing their wrists. The young man in the cell between Don and me provided an opening one day when he stated he'd rather die than spend the rest of his life in prison. I do not believe it was a literal declaration, but Don's eyes probably lit up like a Christmas tree. They passed notes back and forth as Don became his counselor, his mentor, his listening friend.

Just a couple days later, the guard walked up the tier performing the morning count and stopped short just before reaching my cell. I heard his footsteps run back the other way, and within moments our tier was flooded with corrections officers, the captain, medical personnel, and, eventually, a coroner. I heard the cleanup was intense as blood was splattered all over the walls, sink, toilet, and bars. Don was tried for manslaughter, though I do not know the final disposition. I heard there were many notes passed between them along with a long, sharp piece of glass with Don's fingerprints. I can only assume Don spent the rest of his life attempting to be celled next to sad people.

Due to overcrowding we had to double up even in the hole. I was put in with Griswald, a very weird but ingenious guy. Griswald would do things like wipe whole rolls of toilet paper with antiperspirant, create a Bunsen burner donut out of the toilet paper, and light it on fire just to scent our room. These innovations made us feel a little more normal.

One day I was taken out of my cell and put in an interview room. I had no idea what was going on. A few minutes later, two men in suits walked in, sat down across from me, and showed me their secret service credentials. One of them asked me, "Do you think

Griswald could be dangerous to the president of the United States?"

I started to laugh. "Griswald? No way. Not unless he wanted to rub him with a bar of deodorant and set him on fire." I was truly amused.

When I returned to the cell I told Griswald all about my meeting. His eyes lit up! He was visibly excited. "What'd you tell them? Did you say I was crazy?"

"No, of course not. I said you couldn't hurt a flea."

Boy was Griswald pissed. There had been a rumor going around that if you could convince the man that you were crazy they would send you to Western State Hospital. There, your sentence could be dropped and you could get out much quicker. I still don't know if there was any truth to that, but Griswald would have to figure out some other way to demonstrate his insanity other than by sending threatening letters to the president. It was occasions like this that offered bright spots even in segregation.

There were more such events during the six months I spent in the hole. But, again, this book is not about that. The essence of my time in the hole boils down to attempting to answer these questions for myself: *How far down is bottom? Had I reached it? Would I spend the rest of my life becoming accustomed to men raping men, slashing wrists, and spraying blood on prison walls? Did I care any longer what reality each day brought? Did I care about anything anymore? Did anyone care?* I once heard from a good friend of mine that "the bottom is firm." It can take a few minutes to grasp that concept. There is a bottom, and the bottom is firm.

In September 1982, after spending six months in administrative segregation, I was told to wake up at 4:00 a.m. because I was being transferred to Washington State Reformatory in Monroe, Washington. This prison was known as "Gladiator School." Washington Correction Center in Shelton was a country club compared to WSR. I didn't want to go, but I felt I had no choice. I knew my jacket would follow me ("jacket" is the record of incidents occurring in other institutions), but I would simply have to deal with it when the time came. I was a runner. I had been a runner from the moment I hid in the forest behind school in seventh grade. Wherever I was going must always be better than where I just was. I'd figure it out. I was a survivor.

It was an extremely hot day, and the transport from one prison to another—"the chain"—consisted of about twenty guys shackled to each other at the waist and the ankles. We sat on benches lining both sides of the bus. They let us smoke but did not allow open windows. Between the cigarette smoke and the hot sun streaming in through the tiny bus windows, I thought I would literally melt onto the floor. After making stops at a few other jails, we finally drove up the hill to the reformatory. Words like *ominous* and *chilling* came to mind. Some of the guys on the chain had been there before, and they weren't talking much. It's hard to say what was worse—not knowing what we were in for, or knowing all too well.

As the bus entered through the first gate and stopped to be searched underneath, men began to form a wall on the other side of the fence. So much of what Hollywood provides in movies about prison is simply not true or highly exaggerated; but one aspect they do get right is the scene that was unfolding in front of my eyes where men stake their claim on incoming convicts—the fresh meat. They marched us through the inmates surrounding us on each side shouting epithets and sexually explicit desires. I refused to make eye contact. If I had, I might have locked eyes with a particular dirty biker who happened to be expecting me.

We went through the usual intake process, which included fingerprints and a new mug shot. My number would remain the same: 276405. I couldn't believe the prison assigned a woman with an enormous chest, wearing a see-through white blouse to take our pictures. It seemed irresponsible in a setting where a bunch of men who had been deprived of female contact; and it made me mad. I had been chained to men I didn't like in unbearably hot temperatures on a smoke-filled bus for more than half the day. And then they put me in front of this woman as if they were taunting and tempting me. Prison was just a bitch sometimes.

Chapter 7
GLADIATOR SCHOOL

We were filed in to the fish tank. This is where new inmates were housed until they could move into the main population. The only instructions provided by the guard captain we're: 1) don't accept anything for free; 2) don't get into debt; and 3) homosexual activity is not allowed.

Compared to WCC, this prison appeared unstructured. Cells were not assigned; we had to find one. It was our responsibility to find a home amongst 1,000 other inmates. There were some empty two-man cells and there were some two-man cells with only one inmate. Doubling up with someone in a two-man cell was the most likely option. Finding a single guy in a double cell would be difficult. But finding anywhere to live in a cellblock of, to say it delicately, *the same color* was nearly impossible.

WSR consisted of four cellblocks. Each block was four tiers high and forty cells long (except the bottom tier where the showers took up seven cells). The "A" block was purely white and it contained mostly inmates with money. The "B" block was mixed, but relatively calm. The "C" block was almost completely Native American and Latino, and the "D" block was very nearly all African American. Unfortunately for me, at the time, blocks A, B, and C simply did not provide me with any options.

I was not brought up with racist beliefs and I'm certainly not that way today, but two white guys in a block of 153 cells of nearly 100% Black Americans was less than ideal. Yet, this is where we landed. The first night in "D" block, as the inmates gathered their food, ice, and drugs for the evening to the sounds of Marvin Gaye, it could have been just another night on the streets of Harlem.

I adapted fairly well. I knew quite a few guys from King County Jail in Seattle, Shelton, and even MacLaren. And I had a plan. WSR had a music room. I thought if I could just get there and establish a good reputation maybe I could have the backing to withstand the pressures I knew would soon be upon me. I knew I would be tested. Unfortunately, the pressure came before I could set foot in the music room. It came in the form of Steve Baxter, the dirty biker eyeballing me the day I walked through the gauntlet.

The speed of inmate communication both internally at a prison and externally from one institution to another is astounding. Steve Ledbetter knew I was coming to WSR before I did. He was very good friends with Randy Dudrey, president of the weight club at Shelton—the same Randy to whom I still was indebted for $100. Just a few days after I arrived at WSR Steve joined me at mainline (cafeteria) at my four-person table and kindly asked the other two diners to give us some space to talk. Steve was very kind and considerate in his tone as he shared with me his desire for me to have the $100 available within two weeks. He did not detail the consequences should I not meet that target, but somehow he had faith that my own imagination could fill in the gaps.

How in the world would I get $100 within two weeks?

The silver lining in all of this was that I knew at least until I had the money or two weeks had passed I was safe. I had two specific things to be concerned about regarding Steve Ledbetter. Steve was mean, and he knew how to fight. There are many mean convicts but not all of them can back it up. Steve was also a dangerous fighter. Again, fighters who are not mean are not a threat either. But a mean fighter . . . this was a concern.

Finding My Way

I went to the chapel located in the center of the WSR complex. I was not there to find religion or hide out from the main population as so many did. I sought out the chapel because they had a piano. Much like playing the piano at MacLaren or in the basement of an old hotel in Portland, Oregon, it brought me incredible stress relief. When I sat and played a few meaningless chords or even songs out of the hymnal, I had such a sense of calm. The piano was my religion.

I got to know a few of the inmates who had chosen faith as their way of coping with prison life. I did not believe I could take that path with them. The life I started in Springfield, Oregon—where God loved me and I would do my best to love Him back—was over. I'd completely blown that deal.

I arrived at WSR September 7, 1982. Less than two weeks later, on a Sunday evening, I decided to take a walk by myself around the big yard. It was a day just like any other day. I was dealing with the fact that I had no ability to pay back Randy through Steve Ledbetter. Rumors were spreading that I liked black men. Someone had learned I had sold my body in downtown Seattle and turned it into something more than it was. There were also rumors that I had snitched on my crime partners. But these were all in a day's work to me. Boys homes, group homes, jails, juvenile institutions, prisons . . . it all came with the life I had chosen to live. Just another day in prison. I resigned myself that evening to the probability that I would spend the rest of my life this way. I stepped through the gates of the big yard pondering these choices.

I started the counter-clockwise walk on the east side of the track. After twenty yards I looked at the northwest corner where there were about ten tables, each table had four round metal seats. At one of the tables I recognized two men from the chapel. One of them, Max, had shared the salvation message with me on one of the occasions when I played the piano. The two men had their heads bowed, hands folded on the table top. One was quietly talking. They were praying.

Unlike Saul in the Bible, I wasn't on my way to Damascus. But similar to his story I dropped to my knees. My tears flowed freely. I sensed a voice, and it asked me, "Are you done?" I nodded my head and through uncontrollable sobs I responded, "Yes." After another moment I said, "God, if you're willing to take me, I'm yours."

I have no idea if anyone observed the crying twenty-two-year-old man in the big yard that evening. I gathered myself and walked to the chapel where a service was in progress. I found Max later and shared my experience with him. I admitted I was afraid I'd feel differently the next morning, but I had a sense of calm that I had never experienced before. The issues I was having were still there, but I wasn't so afraid of how they might end. If God were as big as He says, should I be worried about anything else? These and other questions were on my mind as I went to sleep that evening. I entered sleep in peace, but morning came without peace. Doubt had edged its way in overnight. My first conscious thought was, *It wasn't real*. Like so many times before, I had a moment of clarity about my sense of separation from God—from my idea of God.

While in jail I had watched a Sunday morning Christian program where Jimmy Swaggart was telling the story of an alcoholic who had sold his daughter's shoes for a bottle. The story had me in tears, praying, "Oh God, I'm so sorry. I know I'm a screw up and your way is the right way." That moment never lasted more than a day or two. And, when I got out of my bunk and my feet hit the floor on this morning, I again felt that the special moment from the evening before had melted away during the night. God was gone. Nothing had changed.

Only, that wasn't entirely true. Standing in front of me outside my cell was my new friend, Max. He simply said, "Dwaine, let's take a walk." We walked and talked about life, God, prison, and salvation. The sensation from my big yard experience returned. I was confident my old life was over. I had a new life and another chance. This felt different. This was different. That day I was able to move into Max's double cell on the first tier of B-block. Also, later that evening I began to meet fellow Christians—Darryl Young, Clay Anderson, Conjouel

Andrews, Donny Burke, Del Denny, Karl MacLaren—and I would spend the next three and a half years with these guys, laughing, crying, fighting, singing, and praying. These were not soft, mealy-mouthed Christians. Each had an incredibly tough life story. Their crimes ranged from murder to child molestation. (Yes, it is true. Men with sex crimes can find solace and redemption in the prison chapel.) I decided on day one that their pasts were none of my business. Is fondling a child worse than turning a man's head into a sea of red using the heavy end of a pool cue? I don't believe I am equipped to make that call.

Plus, I had another problem to deal with. Just a couple days later my brother somehow found it in himself to put $100 on my books. I happily told Steve Ledbetter that I had the money and would be sending it to Randy once I had his "people's" address. But the saga was not over. Steve told me that he would collect the money himself and take care of the payment to Randy. This was a problem. If I gave the money to Steve, my immediate issue would be resolved. However I knew the money would never make it to Randy and my debt would remain unresolved.

My new Christian friends attempted to help. They offered to force Steve into protective custody. Some even offered to hurt him badly so he'd leave me alone. Or, I could still check into protective custody myself. I didn't want the confrontation. I've never been a tough guy. My bravery was nearly always supplemented by weapons and treachery on my side. It reminded me of throwing soap in Chris's eyes at MacLaren. There was no way I could fight Steve and expect anything other than to be on the losing end, perhaps severely, without something to tip the scales in my favor, and I didn't want to be that person anymore.

I'm convinced that not selecting these options and making the correct decision is the reason I am able to write this story today. I had run away my whole life. I had connived, manipulated, cheated, run, and hid in the past rather than standing up to a problem. I knew what I was supposed to do. And that evening I executed that decision.

It was just before lockdown after an evening service in the chapel. Steve's cell was just four cells away from mine on the bottom tier. I walked up to his cell as he was already locked in for the night. I called him over and he stood facing me behind the bars.

"Steve," I started, "Listen man. I can't give you that money. I gotta give it directly to Randy."

Before I could move Steve reached through the bars, grabbed my shirt in his right fist and exploded with a set of expletives. He was completely out of control, and all I could say was "Jesus, Jesus, Jesus, Jesus . . . ." I was able to wrench myself out of his grasp and I turned and walked toward my cell. His screaming followed me. The things he was going to do to me when the bars opened the next morning were things I never knew existed.

Once again, I was physically shaking and I began to wonder if I did the right thing.

A few minutes later, my soon-to-be best friend, Darryl Young, came by and handed me a note on a piece of scratch paper. I opened it. Scrawled on the paper was "Psalm 27:1." I looked it up. It said, "The Lord is my light and my salvation—whom shall I fear? The Lord is the stronghold of my life—of whom shall I be afraid?" And I instantly got it. The fear left. The trembling stopped. My mind was flooded with peace. I did the right thing, and frankly, nothing else mattered. If I walked out of my cell the next morning and Steve dragged me into the south forty (an area that cannot be seen by the guard manning the lock box) and beat the tar out of me, it simply didn't matter. I didn't run. I didn't hide. I was resolved in the fact that whatever happened, happened. God was on my side.

Granted, the next morning when the guard pulled the Johnson bar to unlock all the cell doors on the first tier, I had some trepidation. But I was no longer scared. And sure enough, Steve was waiting for me. But the screaming maniac I pulled away from the night before had become simply a guy in need. He put his arm around me and asked me, hesitantly, "Can I at least have five dollars?" to which I replied, "No. Sorry, Steve."

About three months later when I left my cell one afternoon, Steve approached me cautiously, looking right and left to make sure no one saw him talking to the Christian kid. He leaned in and said with a gruff whisper, "Hey, listen." He looked down for a moment, then, "I'm getting out in a couple of weeks and, to be honest, I'm really scared. See, I have a grandmother who has been praying for me for a long time. I just don't know how to make it out there on the streets. I don't know what to do." Then, he asked something that suddenly made me so weak in the knees I thought I was gonna go down.

Steve asked me, "Will you pray for me?" He was looking right at me, right into my eyes, and his eyes were moist around the edges. If I weren't afraid I'd be written up for homosexual activity I might have given him a hug right then. But I just smiled and answered, "Sure, of course, Steve." And I did. I prayed for the guy who threatened bloody murder if I didn't give him money. But right then, he was just a man who was lost, and who God wanted back. Just like me a few months before.

Steve did return to prison for another short period after his release, but the last I heard was that he was a well-established pastor of a church north of Seattle. There is no darkness that is too dark. There is no deed too dirty. There is no place too far. I have seen the toughest of the tough (by earthly standards) fall to their knees and cry out. Thankfully, God is in the business of welcoming home the prodigal.

The three and a half years after that Sunday evening in September were the best years of my life to that point. I felt free. My circumstances didn't change; I was still in prison. but I was free.

I settled in to do my time with the attitude that this was my city—this was where I lived, played, and worked. I got a job at the GED Learning Center provided by Edmonds Community College in Lynnwood, Washington. There were more men learning their ABCs than there were preparing for their GED. I took attendance and assisted with their studies. The biggest perk, besides the $30 per month salary, was the tape duplication machine. Sometimes, as a favor, sometimes for a couple dollars' worth of commissary, I would make copies of music tapes for other inmates. Overall it was a very good gig—certainly much better than working in the kitchen or the laundry.

One day a few large boxes were brought in to the classroom. They were computers—TRS-80 to be exact. I knew absolutely nothing about them. There was a monitor and a keyboard, and they were pretty much useless until we hooked up a tape machine and loaded a program into the computer. A math question appeared on the screen, "What is 7 x 7?" The student would type "49" and then the screen responded with "Correct!" This was called CAI or Computer Aided Instruction.

A couple of days after the computers arrived I was so intrigued I started the computer up to see if I could make it work. All I got was a blinking question mark. I realized I could type in that field, so I typed my name and hit the "Enter" key. It responded with "Syntax error!" I thought, *What's wrong with my name!?* While I didn't understand much, I did eventually figure out that I could write a program to accomplish something. For instance, I could write a program that would convert standard to metric or calculate how much I was paying for gas. None of these ideas seemed interesting to me, but I did take daily attendance and figured I could write a program to help with that. So I did. And like falling on my knees in the big yard deeply impacted my life and who I was, programming the computer to solve problems would seriously aid in my ability to make a living and have a career. I had to land in prison to start my life.

Making a Future

There was a different service in the chapel every night of the week, and twice on Saturday and Sunday. We considered our main weekly service to be the Full Gospel Business Men on Saturday night. All of us were novices in the faith, but anyone who had been attending and studying the Bible for a year was considered a senior pastor. Our influences were many, but Kenneth Hagin, Kenneth Copeland, and Keith Greene were dominant.

Sadly, we understood the concept of grace the least. It was as if we assuaged our guilt over our crimes by embracing a total lack of tolerance of any sin. Lukewarm was the enemy. Every day we were reminded of the life we came from and the life waiting for us if we stepped a foot off the straight and narrow path.

This philosophy was illustrated very well one Saturday evening during the worship service. Karl Peterson was leading us in the thousandth time singing "I've Got a River of Life," and I was providing the piano accompaniment. In the middle of the song, Del Denny walked up the aisle with a frail boy, no older than seventeen. Earlier in the day, Karl had asked Del not to bring this kid to the chapel. He was a sinner— he had been performing sex acts with other prisoners for protection—and sinners need not come unless they were ready to repent. Del felt differently and demonstrated this by bringing the kid to church anyway. As the worship song concluded, Karl motioned to me to continue playing as he stepped off the platform. He gave the "Come follow me" signal to Del and they both walked down the aisle between the pews. They could have been two guys on their way to get some ice cream for as casual as it seemed. They were only outside the chapel doors for a few seconds. Karl came back in first, and shortly behind him, Del followed, holding his hand to his face to catch the blood pouring from his nose. Del took his place back in the pew beside the kid. Karl returned to the platform, gave me the nod and I began the introduction to the next song. This was Christianity at its best in Washington State Reformatory.

There were two Christian bands and each asked me to play piano and guitar and to sing. Karl played amazing drums and had a beautiful voice (and a nice right jab). Conjouel played bass. They were both uncomfortable sharing me with the other band and invited me to the chapel to "pray" about it. In the back room of the chapel Conjouel bowed his head and placed his hand on my head and began to pray in a "thus sayeth the Lord" manner. As his words became more direct with implications that God, speaking through him, was telling me it was their band and their band only with which I would participate, Conjouel began to push down on my head. I realized he was attempting to convince me that I was to be "slayed in the spirit." I put my right foot back a few inches to balance myself against the force of his pressure. He began to pray louder and the pressure increased. I put my right foot back even more and leaned forward against the downward pressure. I refused to be taken down. This continued until finally Conjouel gave up. After the *Amen* I looked like a football lineman protecting the quarterback with all his might. Later I asked Conjouel why he tried to push me down with his hand. He simply replied, "I never touched you." Of course not.

We prayed and studied the Bible together almost every day. A "mature" Christian in prison might only have six months in the faith. It didn't take much to feel superior to some and inferior to others. One Saturday evening, a young inmate was sharing with us about his decisions and how he would make them based on specific occurrences, otherwise known as "putting out the fleece." For instance, if he were struggling with whether he should take a job in the prison laundry, receiving a letter from his mother on Tuesday was his sign that God was giving the thumbs up. Being the much more mature Christian, I sat him down and shared that putting out the fleece showed a lack of faith and that God wants us to trust in our sense of how the Holy Spirit was leading us. I returned to my cell that night feeling rather smug in my wisdom. But, as I lay on my mattress with the lights out, God impressed upon me a message of His own. I sensed He said, "Who are you to tell me how I can communicate with my children?" My inner self churned from the reality of this correction. As I grew in my spiritual life, I felt this disciplining over and over again, and I'm grateful for it.

For the time we were together, these men were my support system, my confidantes, my friends, and my family. We often talked about how our lives would be different on the outside now that we had a relationship with God. Some of the men got the opportunity to try only to fail and end up back inside, others died as a result of their inability to bear the burdens of life outside the strictures of an institution.

Donny Burke had been convicted of attempting to rob a pharmacy. The pharmacist recognized Don, wrestled the revolver away from him, and shot him in the leg. The police found Don buried under hallmark greeting cards and toilet paper, held down by pharmacy patrons. After getting out of prison in 1985, he was re-incarcerated shortly after getting addicted to heroin again.

Del Denny (or "Mugsy" as he was known in Walla Walla) was an incredibly intelligent man. He talked to me for hours and hours about recovery from drugs and emotional pain. I didn't understand a lot of what he said, but I think it did him good to just talk about it. Del told me we needed to replace our desire to get out of prison with another faith picture or we would end up in a vicious cycle of release and return. Del was a career criminal and had spent 80% of his life behind bars. He got out of prison in 1987 only to return to heroin. He shot a drug dealer after robbing him, got caught, and was sent back to prison. The only witness, a prostitute, refused to testify so Del got out of prison on a Friday evening. He did not live another twenty-four hours before his body succumbed to an overdose of cocaine.

Another friend, Shawn McDowell, who had everything in the world going for him—looks, body, and brains—got out in 1987 and took a job as a bouncer at a nude dancing club. One day, after we both got out, I saw him riding his bike on a Saturday afternoon in Seattle. That evening he was on the news after attempting to rob a grocery store in northeast Seattle. Of eight stores it was the only one he had not robbed twice and the police were waiting for him. I'd spent many hours playing Cribbage with Shawn in prison and he told me more than once that he would never allow himself to be sent back. He was true to his word. When the police told Shawn to drop his weapon he lifted his revolver and was cut down at near point blank range with a 12-guage shotgun.

Darryl Young was my best friend and mentor—the one who brought me scriptures the night I told Steve he would not receive money from me. Within a week after that incident I moved into Darryl's cell and we were cellmates for over a year. On one hand, Darryl was as close to normal as anyone else I knew, including the guards and prison staff. He was extremely articulate and spoke with authority. He studied the Bible extensively and could teach and preach like a seasoned pastor. No matter what drama or chaos occurred in the chapel, Darryl was always quick to remind me, "Dwaine, it's not our church. It's God's church." He worked as the Chapel Outreach worker and was never at a loss for convicts in need of help. On the other hand, Darryl was a seasoned convict. Ten years older than I, he had spent a good portion of his life in juvenile and adult prisons. He knew how to do time and carried himself in such a way that most people felt it was inadvisable to cross him. He was both loving and dangerous. When Darryl hugged you he put his face right up next to yours as he genuinely cared for you and you knew it.

One man chose to cross Darryl for a brief moment and it nearly cost him his life. Steve Crawford was eighteen years old and was sentenced to life in prison.

A tall, lanky kid, Steve had attempted an escape from a juvenile institution in Washington State, during which he hit a guard with a hammer and killed him. Before his life had really had a chance to get started it was over. As one would expect, he dealt with serious self-esteem issues and was trying to find his path as a young lifer. He wandered into the chapel one day and we took him in, sharing our faith and hope. Edward Stokes was labelled as one of the worst sex offenders on the west coast. He admitted to molesting over 200 boys and had been convicted of sodomy and kidnapping. His parents owned a mortuary, and whether it was the cause or just the convenience, Ed was caught more than once having sex with the dead bodies. Making matters worse, Ed's intelligence was way above average and if you didn't know about him and simply had a casual conversation with him, you might think he was a college professor. Ed also knew the Bible backward and forward. He loved hanging out at the chapel to share his "faith" with the young boys who came to the chapel looking for safety, love, and nurturing.

Edward Stokes and Steve Crawford became good friends. They began to spend a lot of their time together. Ed gained Steve's trust by being a good listener, especially to Steve's story of being adopted. They studied the Bible together and prayed. Soon Ed asked Steve if he wanted to share a cell. Steve asked Darryl and me what we thought and we did our best to talk him out of it. Ed capitalized on this and drew Steve away from us, convincing him that we did not understand their close friendship. They moved in to a cell on the second tier, just above our cell. There was nothing we could do.

Within just a couple of weeks we noticed a change in Steve. He stopped coming to the chapel and averted his eyes when we walked by. Darryl was eventually able to get Steve alone and he got the full story. At night when the bars closed for the day, Ed would make Steve sit naked in a bucket of ice. He would then wrap a sock around Steve's neck and choke him just enough to make him black out, at which point Ed would sodomize him. Afterward, Ed would tell him that he loved him and they'd read scriptures together. The next night he would repeat the ritual. And the next.

When Steve was asked if he wanted to move out of the cell, he said he was too scared and Ed would never go for that. Darryl asked him again, "Do you want your own cell?" Steve finally broke down and agreed.

As the Chapel Outreach Worker, one of Darryl's responsibilities was coordinating cell changes with the captain. These cell changes would occur about thirty minutes before dinner. It was generally a very quiet time on the block. Doors would open and the cell moves would begin. On this particular afternoon Darryl was let out of our cell first and he made his way up one flight of stairs to the second tier. I heard his footsteps getting louder as he walked up to Ed and Steve's cell. I couldn't see, but I heard the Johnson bar pulled down and their single cell door was unlatched. I heard Ed say something to the effect of this move was not needed or it wasn't going to happen, challenging Darryl who was standing in their cell doorway. The momentary silence before Darryl spoke was deafening. Darryl's words were chilling. "Make a move and they'll be carrying you out of here today in a box." It wasn't boisterous. It wasn't a threat. It was just matter of fact. Years of prison, a convict mentality, and priorities determined by genuine love for others nearly culminated in the death of one man and life in prison for another. There was no question that Darryl would have followed through.

For this and other reasons, I had put Darryl on a pedestal, and in every story that is never a good thing. Darryl eventually was released due to a technicality— they used his juvenile record in his trial. Having John Henry Brown, a notoriously good attorney, on his side didn't hurt. Learning of the things Darryl did when he was out and his personal struggles hit me pretty hard. I began to question everything. Is this real? Are stories of throwing the Bible into the garbage on the way out the door true? I stayed angry with Darryl for years until I understood that he didn't put himself up as an example for me to live; I put him there.

There are others God used, both positive and negative, to get me through the remainder of my sentence. A few of them are doing well. Most are dead or back in prison. Many of the things I saw and experienced in prison will be with me forever. I would like to forget some of them, but I cannot. They happened. There are far too many experiences, both horrible and tremendously valuable, to record in a single book. I never set out for this book to be about prison, or everything else that led up to my incarceration. The real story begins on April 10, 1986 when I walked away from Madison House Work Release a free man.

Dan and Helen

In all of my time in institutions I learned not to trust church volunteers. The truth is, going into prison as a group of Christians for an outreach event is strictly for their benefit, not the prisoners'. I've heard many men brag about how they made friends with the toughest cons and, of course, were not afraid of them, which is completely ridiculous and dishonest. But the worst volunteers were the ones who were only satisfied if they could go home and tell their church and friends that they led a convict through the "Sinner's Prayer" or helped a desperate inmate in some dramatic way. I had one returning volunteer ask me how I was doing. I told him the truth. I said I was fine. He came in a little closer, leading with a very sad face, dipped his chin down, lifted his eyebrows and asked again, "How are you really doing?" Again, I said everything was great and I was having a great day. He backed up, shook his head, and said angrily, "I don't believe you!" He walked away without a story to tell.

Dan and Helen seemed different. In 1984 they came into our prison with a group called Prison Fellowship started by Chuck Colson. Helen was fifty-three and Dan about ten years older. Helen had been a missionary in Japan for many years. Dan was a long-time Boeing employee. I don't know what drew us together; perhaps it was my confidence that I would make it on the outside. I saw that they were faithful and they came across very genuine, like they were truly there for us and not just themselves. I began to look forward to their visits and we began to develop a special friendship in spite of my very small trust zone.

As January of 1985 rolled around I became eligible to go to the Honor Farm. I still had over a year on my sentence, but this would be the first step toward my release. By now, Helen was sending me greeting cards in the mail once or twice a week. They were nice and inspiring. I rarely reciprocated, which she brought up in a conversation, suggesting I do so. I had just two visits from family in prison in five years, so it was nice to have someone to talk to.

The Monroe State Honor farm supplied local schools and institutions with milk and ice cream. It was a fully-functioning dairy, and each day they milked 150 cows. I moved from a cell behind a wall and gun towers to a dorm room where I could walk away if I chose. I wasn't used to walking outside at night or the freedom of movement. It felt awkward, as if at any moment I could be shot.

I ran garbage detail for a couple of weeks, then got to work in the farm office filling out purchase orders on a typewriter. I thought maybe when I got out for good I could go to work in an office instead of slaving over a hot grill as a cook as most ex-cons did. There were no computers in the farm office when I was there, but I felt I could use one if I had to.

Over the next year I would work in every position on the dairy farm, including driving the tractor and front loader. I had a couple of pet cats, although one died of distemper. I did whatever I could to try to feel normal. I put Dan and Helen on my visitor list as soon as I could. I also added a nice young lady I'd met while on the inside. Shelley was a volunteer at a function at which some of the guys and I shared our testimonies. They were videotaped by the Catholic Arch Diocese of Seattle. She was cute and we'd written back and forth a few times, but Helen cautioned me against it, advising that it would not be a good idea for me to get into a relationship before I was fully released.

It just happened that Shelley was approved for visiting before Dan and Helen, so Shelley was the first to visit me at the Honor farm. She and I had a very nice visit and I actually thought maybe there could be a future with her, though she certainly had not done or said anything to indicate she felt the same way. Having been incarcerated as long as I had, I didn't trust my own judgment. I could easily interpret her breathing as a sign of interest.

My next conversation with Helen on the phone didn't go well. Helen was upset and accused me of using them and that I would kick them to the curb when I was released. She shared a story of how her adopted family never truly accepted her. My visit with Shelly somehow related to this experience for her, although I didn't understand how. I was torn. But I made a rash decision. I told Shelly I couldn't see her anymore, which made Helen happy.

Dan and Helen would visit me on Sundays and bring me big bags of snacks. On the inside, or "up on the hill," I had one visit from my parents. Now I was getting weekly visits and snacks. I began to feel valuable. Shortly after my arrival at the farm Helen began to visit me on her own without Dan every Tuesday evening. We would walk around the yard and talk. I also began to talk with Helen on the phone every evening. A couple of my friends raised questioning eyebrows, but I told them the truth: we were just close friends and I had absolutely no question that our relationship was on the up and up. I resented these accusations and innuendoes. In fact, Helen introduced me to her niece, Susan, also my age. I believed Helen was hoping for a match.

One day Helen and I were walking and talking about life and nonsense on a spring evening and at some point we stopped and she gave me a hug. It wasn't the first time. She'd hugged me before in front of Dan and the Honor farm staff. But this time my body responded quite unexpectedly in a very noticeable way. It made sense in that I'd been in prison for a long time, but I was so incredibly embarrassed. I fell all over myself apologizing and reassured Helen that I had absolutely no feelings for her in that way. After all, I was a Christian now and she was married, nearly twenty-six years older than I was, and a Christian herself.

That evening I got on my knees and prayed and asked for forgiveness. In my mind, I may as well have smoked a joint. I called Helen that evening and again made it clear that I had no bad intentions. I certainly did not want her sexually. Helen was quite upset, but not for the reasons I expected. It took me a minute to grasp her complaint. It was my adamant apology she didn't like. Granted, of course, she said there would be no sexual connection, because that would be wrong; but, she was offended that I did not acknowledge that was even in the realm of possibility. I was too adamant, she said. What was so wrong with her? I pondered this and finally gave into its logic. Perhaps I could have been less emphatic in my apology. So, I apologized for the offensive apology and moved on. And Helen was once again happy.

In the summer of my year at the Honor farm I was asked to attend a class for drug addiction and alcoholism. I resented this because I felt that I no longer had a drug or alcohol problem. There were always plenty of drugs in prison and opportunity was always there. To entertain such a thought that I could still have these issues was to me a lack of faith. I refused to give in, no matter how it was presented by the drug and alcohol counselors. I finished the class without a certificate because acknowledgement of having a problem was a requirement for completion.

I went in front of the parole board in the fall of 1985 and heard the words I had been waiting for since I'd turned myself in nearly five years earlier. I was approved for release. I would first go to Pre-release in Tacoma for processing to a Work Release facility and then be released on parole at a time determined by the parole board the following year. I allowed myself to believe I would actually be leaving prison. The purposeful mind set I adopted, that prison would be my life, was a difficult thing to break. It was also dangerous. Somehow I knew I could not wait until my release date to begin thinking like a civilian again. But thinking and feeling as though I were already out created conflict with some of the guards and inmates. It's an attitude called short-timers disease and is perceived by others as your acting better than they are. Getting into a fight or getting written up by guards could undo all of my hard work. This transitional period is the most vulnerable time for a convict.

But, I did survive, and on January 5, 1986 I sat on a bus being transferred to Tacoma Pre-Release. There were no chains or leg irons. I had a couple boxes of clothes, a plant, and a guitar. I was nervous, scared, and thrilled all at the same time. I had heard it would be a couple of weeks before transfer to a work release and I knew those two weeks would be brutally slow.

The Tacoma Pre-Release facility was on the Western Washington State Hospital grounds in Steilacoom, Washington. We each had our own room with a nice bed and a dresser. Dan and Helen drove down from their house on Green Lake in Seattle and it was so nice to visit without feeling like we were in an institutional setting.

During the first week we filled out an endless flow of paper work and were required to attend vocational training class. The emphasis was on drafting a résumé and getting our food handlers license. I strongly pushed back on this requirement as well. The teacher, a young lady about thirty years old, told me that I needed this to fall back on should I not have the opportunity to work in an office as I hoped. For a few days I refused and she and I got into some fairly heated discussions. I wanted a pass. I wanted a waiver. Taking the food handlers class, in my eyes, was a sign of weakness. I had absolutely no intentions of failing. And even more so, I believed the teacher simply didn't know what to do with someone who believed as much as I did in my success. Perhaps she was jaded. Maybe one day, if she reads this book, we can meet over coffee. But in the end, I took the class to prevent being sent back to Monroe. And I must admit that it is a good thing to know that bacteria begins to grow on food left out for four hours in over 40° F.

Helen visited me on her own during my second week at the pre-release facility. At the end of the visit she gave me a hug and instead of the usual peck on my cheek, Helen planted one on my lips and hung it there for about three seconds. Long seconds. I was stunned. I know I didn't imagine it. The more I thought about it the angrier I got. I called her that evening and confronted her with, "What was that?"

And again her response was surprising. She became angry with me. She denied it and said I was just trying to find a reason to bail on our relationship. I was using that as an excuse to leave them once I was paroled. This always happens to her, she said. I began to wonder if I had misinterpreted Helen's innocent gesture. I was simply too high strung and needed to relax. Everything was fine once I apologized. She accepted the apology and was happy once again.

After two weeks at Pre-Release in Tacoma I was transferred to the Madison House Work Release facility in the Central District of Seattle just off 21st and Madison. I could see out of my bedroom window across the street at the front of the local store and watch the drug deals, one after another. The big pressure at Work Release is that it costs $10 per day to stay there. Every day without a job resulted in going further into the red, yet we were not allowed to leave to look for a job for two days. The third day arrived and I signed myself out after Helen drove up to take me on my first day of freedom. I walked out the front door, got into the passenger side of her blue Volkswagen hatchback, and we drove away.

My feelings of euphoria were tempered by the need to find a job quickly. We drove into downtown Seattle and I dropped off my résumés at Kelly Services and General Employment, two placement agencies specializing in office administration resources. We drove to Pike Place Market and had lunch. The Donut Shop on first and Pike had been replaced by a T-shirt store. As we rounded Pike Street onto South 2nd Street I looked at the building on the corner that used to be the Association disco. It was here that adults converged to take advantage of underage kids. I had been one of the abused. Maybe coincidence, or maybe by the hand of God, I watched a large rat stealthily crawl out from under the barred front door, sniff the sidewalk for a moment, and then disappear under some rubbish. I think God wanted me to see it for what it was: an inviting teenage dance hall on the outside filled with nasty old rats on the inside.

We drove north on Aurora to Green Lake where I got to see the house to which I would be paroled. Helen had already purchased sheets, linens, window coverings, and other knick-knacks that would make me feel at home. I was grateful. No one had ever gone out of their way so much for me. Across the street was a beautiful lake with constant foot traffic. We just sat and talked together. I wanted to enjoy it, but I'd imagined this for so many years that it just felt surreal. Would I open my eyes and find myself back in the big yard, fantasizing once again about a day that would never come? In my heart I was still incarcerated. I simply could not connect with the reality that I could stop at a store and purchase some Fritos. It would take some time for that awkward disconnect to release me.

A short time later, Helen drove me back to Madison House Work Release and dropped me off with a promise to come back and pick me up the next day. This was a tough moment. I really didn't like it there. I had a taste of freedom from institutional rules and boundaries only to be swimming back with the sharks. The men were no different here than in the joint—angry, predatory, violent—but curbing their morbid delights just long enough to convince men and women in suits that they had changed their ways. I kept to myself and waited for the next day when Helen's blue Volkswagen would arrive.

I was called back to both General Employment and Kelly Services to take some typing and writing tests. I did well with both and was told I would be placed as soon as an opportunity came along. I received a call back from Kelly Services first. Helen drove me to the building on 2nd and Seneca and dropped me off. I took the elevator up to their floor as quickly as I could. I was so excited; I was going to prove that vocational teacher wrong today. Kelly Services informed me that I was accepted as a data entry clerk at a large insurance company and would receive $6 per hour. This was more than a cook's job! I was an office worker! I filled out some paperwork and waited a few minutes for them to finalize logistics with the company. I took the elevator to the lobby and was so excited I could barely get the words out to Helen that I got my first office job. We hugged and I went back upstairs. When I walked back in their demeanor had changed. They sat me down and asked me if I was in fact at a work-release facility. Of course I said I was. It was a requirement that we tell any potential employer that we were in work release, but I never thought it would impact my ability to be hired.

Unfortunately, because I was technically hired by Kelly Services, but not directly supervised by them, I could not be employed by Kelly Services. It was simply their policy. My heart sank, and I walked out of their office hurt, confused, and angry. I had the skills. What else mattered? I prayed, but out of frustration. In my mind, I had done bad things and received bad things as a result. Now I was doing good things. Why weren't the good things happening to me? My immaturity was the loudest voice in the room. I was mentally ready for the big bad devil regarding drugs, alcohol, and sex. I would say NO! I was not prepared to face the pain that came from rejection and disappointment. I fully expected things to go my way now that I was free. I had a lot to learn about navigating life on the outside without my default responses and crutches.

On one of the early days at Work Release, Helen picked me up during the day and we ended up at their house alone. We were in the small family room with the TV and small desk where Dan worked on their bills. The conversation somehow moved to cancer and then breast cancer. Helen nonchalantly told me that she at one time had a benign lump removed from her breast. *Okay*, I thought, *good to know, I guess*. Then, without any warning, Helen lifted her sweater and bra, exposing her whole breast, and showed me the scar where the doctor removed the lump.

My mind began to replay our history together. I was sure I had misread Helen's anger for seeing Shelley Schmidt before her at the Honor farm. My overstated denial of ever seeing Helen in a sexual way was clearly hurtful. I had made too much of Helen's three-second peck in Pre-Release. But, there were signs in all of her reactions. And, now, when I saw her breast as we sat alone during the middle of the day at her house, I consciously made the decision to have an affair with Helen Jacobsen. She was my best friend. She took me places. She bought me things. I kissed her that day, and she kissed me back. I brought up the fact that my faith was important and questioned, "Doesn't God object to adultery?" "Yes," she said, "but God understands." I bought it because I was naïve about this new faith and because I needed to.

Soon after, I finally got hired through the employment placement agencies. When I had to tell anyone that I was in work release and just spent five years in prison, I looked them in the eye and asked, "How would you like to be part of a success story?" This approach rarely failed. And I found out that compared to others with the same skills that I was better than most. I always felt I had more to prove. I went to one data entry position and finished in one hour what was supposed to take four. I was excited to see I got paid for all four hours. I took whatever small successes I had and made them into self-image growing experiences. When it came to what I did for a living, I had significant maturity. But when it came to life experiences, social interactions, and emotional heavy lifting, I was no better than a fourteen-year-old at a high school dance. I was awkward. I certainly never felt like I fit in, especially at church. The college and career class at Calvary Christian Assemblies of God worked hard at accepting me. I did find that a couple of young men who I thought were timid and weak were, in fact, strong Christian men. I didn't want to be judged by my cover, but was often quick to judge others. My meter was prison gauge and it would take years to change that.

One young lady at church took a liking to me. She

began to call me to ask me out for coffee. Helen told me that she was being much too aggressive and pushy. Eventually the calls calls stopped and my inappropriate relations with Helen progressed. By March I was allowed to spend nights at Dan and Helen's. In the morning after Dan left we were intimate, but Helen stopped short of intercourse. On one of these occasions I told Helen, "You know that this will eventually ruin our friendship." And she agreed, but we had already gone too far. Sometime after arriving in Work Release, but before being paroled on April 10, 1986, Helen and I had sex. After our first time Helen said that while it was wrong, God understood that we loved each other. My immaturity allowed me to hang on to that ridiculous statement as though it were true just to assuage my guilt around Dan.

Before and after parole, Helen and I went out at night. Once I wanted to go to the airport so we could just watch the planes take off and land. Sometimes we'd go to a lounge in downtown Seattle and listen to live music. I would have one or two beers. We would also hang out at Dilettante's on Broadway in Capitol Hill. Once we noticed a couple of young girls around my age were listening in and laughing along with our conversation. They were very cute and obviously interested in me. I liked the attention, but Helen was really bothered by it and whispered how rude they were. I had no ability to compartmentalize my relationship with her, though Helen did not seem to have a problem doing this.

She was married. She slept with Dan every night and remained the "good" wife while I refused opportunities with other women in an effort to remain loyal to her.

During the last few weeks of my incarceration I spent nearly all my time at Dan and Helen's, so when I paroled on April 10th it was not much different from any other day. The only variation from my routine was that I went down to Green Lake by myself, sat on the concrete steps, and cried. I may have cried because I thought I was supposed to. It had been ten years since the day my mom and dad dropped me off at the Children's Services Division. I had spent seven of those ten years incarcerated. When this part of my life started I was sixteen, but had the emotional and mental capabilities of someone much younger. I started out angry and got much angrier. Now I wondered if my commitment to following Jesus had tempered my anger or simply covered it up. Did I understand enough of God's plan and blessings in spiritual places to believe I had value or was I hanging on by the thread of hope I found in my new computer skills? And now that I no longer smoked pot or took drugs, now that I went to church and had no interest in robbing people, could I actually live on the outside as a Christian? What about the fact that I was in an adulterous relationship with a woman twice my age while her husband sat in another room just ten feet away? Had I really changed at all?

Chapter 8
ADAPTING TO REAL FREEDOM

I convinced myself early on that my struggles were not related to the adjustment to getting out of prison. They were the same struggles everyone had—how to make ends meet, who to trust, how to get along with others. I heard about ex-convicts who had issues finding work. While I did lose a couple of opportunities specifically because of my past, there was always another possibility waiting for me around the corner. I figured as long as I had a positive outlook about this, I could deal with the rest because it was just part of life.

My first real full-time employment was at a company called Program for Appropriate Technology in Health. Essentially I was a secretary for one of the directors. I transcribed dictation, edited documents, and did filing. My salary was $14,000 per year, and I thought I landed on a gold mine. My initial goal never changed: to be the best at my job. My competition was a young lady around my age. She tried numerous times to get me to go out, but I simply wasn't interested. Then she turned on me. I also discovered she had been learning about a computer called the Apple McIntosh. When she saw me sitting at this computer one day she immediately told my boss that I wasn't authorized to use this piece of equipment. This was my first encounter with office territorialism. I didn't get it. I thought the more we all knew the better off the company would be.

I began to realize there were rules in this world that I just didn't understand. For instance, one time I took a sick day and stayed home. I went to the mall and bought a very nice black wool winter coat. I really thought I looked good. The next day at work I was showing it off to my coworkers and boss. I said, "Look what I bought yesterday on my sick day!" The reaction was odd— they just looked at each other. Later that morning my boss took me into her office and explained to me that sick days were to be used for sickness. I adamantly disagreed. I told her I had earned the sick day and it was mine to use however I wanted. I also showed up late for work frequently. I always felt I left with enough time, but sometimes the Fremont drawbridge was raised and I certainly did not feel that was my fault. Again my boss and I argued in her office. I just didn't understand how five or ten minutes made a difference.

I had the talent but not the mental or emotional maturity to operate successfully in society. When I thought I was right I was like a dog with a bone. I could not let loose of it. I can only imagine the combination of capability without maturity was difficult for those around me. It's a good thing I was likeable—a personality trait I had honed over years of surviving in dangerous situations.

After six months, I found a job as a word processor at a law firm, Ferguson & Burdell. I was paid $13 per hour as a contractor to transcribe dictation. While I was there I discovered a database that was used to store information to support a large anti-trust action against movie distributors. It was called "RBase System V." The database resource (DB) asked me if I could enter some data. In the process I quickly learned how to perform other administrative operations such as creating new menus, data tables, and CRUD (Create, Update, and Delete) operations. Within a short time I was able to take over the database and I supplied the attorneys with the information they needed during the litigation. My dream of programming computers instead of washing dishes or cooking in a restaurant had been realized.

I found many opportunities to design and develop software for the legal and professional services industry. I was able to do this because the Mac and PC were still relatively new and there were not enough skilled resources who knew what questions to ask in an interview. Whenever the job opportunity required using a technology new to me, I always responded the same: "Yup, I can do that." I would just learn it quickly and deliver successfully most of the time.

On one occasion I almost didn't succeed. Kelly Services sent me to a law firm that needed a 1099 program for capturing their vendors and expenditures. They asked me to use a database program called "dBase." They had not yet installed it but had the program and an instruction manual. I managed to install it in a PC (XT) but simply could not grasp how to use it. After three days I sat down with Lucille, the accounting manager who hired me, and with my head hanging told her that I couldn't do it. They were throwing their money away. Lucille looked at me across her desk. She was close to retirement and had been working for this law firm for many years. After a long pause she leaned forward and said, "Dwaine, I think you can do this. Keep going. I'll worry about the law firm's money." And that was that. At approximately midnight that same day the lights went on and I understood the things I needed to do in order to write the program using dBase. This is what's known as the learning curve. It would always come, but I had to persevere through "not knowing" before the "knowing" occurred. I will be forever grateful to Lucille for not letting me give up on myself because dBase is the foundation of most of the software I would develop for the next twelve years.

I did have my share of failures. I severely underbid projects, and it wasn't until many years later that I started estimating based on my actual value. But I also knew that I needed the experience, so one day when an outstanding opportunity came available, I had the experience to draw on.

BREAKING UP

Helen and I continued our illicit affair from the date of my parole until I moved to California just over three years later. Helen, Dan, and I were a family. We went to church together, went out to restaurants together, and went on many vacations together. Whether we went camping or on a road trip and stayed at hotels, our arrival routine was always the same. Soon after we got everything unpacked Dan would leave to go on a walk or hike and Helen and I would have sex. At the time I just considered it good fortune that we never got caught. But now I realize that was not the case. I was taking care of something that Dan would not or could not take care of. This was verified one evening when Helen and I were lying on my bed, making out, legs entwined. Somehow we didn't hear the creak of the stairs until Dan was standing in my bedroom doorway. We looked up from our horizontal position and instead of Dan becoming angry, he quickly backed up, said he was sorry, and went back downstairs. Yet, whether by my own immaturity or subconscious denial, I just couldn't believe that a man who knew someone was banging his wife was indifferent about it.

There were numerous times during that three years when I told Helen we needed to stop. Many times it was the result of a convicting sermon. I would walk down the aisle to the altar and cry out in shame and guilt. I would tell Helen that we could no longer have a sexual relationship, regardless of how awkward that would be. Even though she voiced agreement, I knew she would not quit. The next morning instead of leaving my bed and joining Helen in hers I would stay upstairs, shower, and dress. Walking downstairs I could hear her crying. Loudly. Sobbing, really. Almost a low wail. And I loved her. So I would go to console her. And it would start all over again.

In 1988 I connected with a woman who had been married to my dad's best friend in college named Sara. She was ten years older than me and she was hot. She had two teenage children who were just babies when I met her. Once, I drove to Oregon to visit her as I was beginning to develop some feelings. The next day, when I returned home, I parked my car behind the house and came in through the back door to the kitchen. There was incredibly shrill wailing coming from the basement. It was loud, crying prayer, something like, "Oh God, save him from himself. Keep him away from the devil's grasp." And so on. I realized she was praying for me. Or at least the words indicated that I was the focus of her wailing. But I began to understand that day that it wasn't as much for me as much as it was for her. She didn't want to lose what she had. For the first time, I really saw the possessiveness and the hypocrisy in Helen. Granted, I should have seen it much sooner, but I was blind because I loved her.

Another trend I noticed was that whenever I went out with another woman or suggested we curb our sexual activities, Helen would bring up how much money I owed. Sometimes I didn't make enough to pay the $350 rent or I would borrow money to by computer supplies. Later I learned the "gifts" were not gifts at all. They were loans I was to pay back once our relationship ended.

The unraveling came in July 1989. Helen had an aunt who owned the deed on some church property in Japan that she sold for six million dollars. Helen let it slip that her aunt wanted to give some of that cash to Dan and her but would not make the contribution as long as I was living there. That made me realize Dan and Helen's portrayal of me to their extended family was less than exceptional. I was seen as a burden, or even worse, someone taking advantage of their kindness. I felt like a prostitute once again. I still loved Helen, despite the thawing of my blindness, and I knew it was time to go. I could not live there as a friend and roommate. Helen simply would not allow that.

I have great memories of my time with Dan and Helen—of camping and fishing trips, of riding my motorcycle and visiting places like Fort St. John in northern British Columbia and the Grand Canyon in Arizona. I had a great place to live on Greenlake and the opportunity to be a first-time entrepreneur without fear of going hungry. And I grew up a little through my relationships with them; but it was time to go. The guilt over what I was doing with Helen was too much to live with any longer. In August of 1989 I left, and did so with Dan's blessing.

Moving On

In just over three years I had gained significant software development skills, including design and analysis. I had cultivated a nice list of successful clients and began to hone a special skill of communicating technical concepts to non-technical people. I realized not everyone had that. The funny thing is, the foundation for this skill came from having to communicate to survive on the city streets and while hitchhiking around the country. I could sell myself to new clients in an office the way I used to sell myself to new clients on the street.

I moved in with my parents who had relocated to Thousand Oaks, California. I felt that I had proven to them and myself that I had changed for the good permanently. I desperately wanted the relationship with them that I never had and naively thought my mom and dad had the ability to reciprocate. It was awkward at best, and just as when I was in high school I did my best to stay away from them.

Four months later on January 6, 1990 I was walking up the aisle at the Chapel of Love in Las Vegas holding the hand of Grace Munro. She and her two girls, Lisa (9) and Shannon (13), lived in the condo just behind my parents in Thousand Oaks, California. Grace and I met and instantly gravitated toward each other like two sick people hoping the other had the antidote.

I had a good job making $20 per hour as a software developer in downtown Las Angeles at the LA County Municipal Court. My self-esteem was completely wrapped up in how much money I made and what I did for a living. Grace had been married and divorced three times. She did not have her high school diploma and had no skills other than retail sales. I married her because I believed marriage was the quickest way to land in "normal." I liked being a hero. It made me feel valuable to provide for a family. And, I liked the idea of being a parent. It made a lot of sense to me at the time.

Within days of starting to date Grace I began to exhibit extremely controlling behavior. It started out as jealousy. During our third date at a fancy sushi restaurant I saw Grace talking with some guys as I exited the restroom. She tossed her head back and laughed at something one of them had said. I felt immediate rage. I knew what these guys wanted from her, but what could she want from them? Were they better looking? Were they wealthy? Did they have something I didn't? When I got her away from the group I asked her, tight lipped and angry, "Why are you talking to them? Did you want to party with them? Sleep with them?"

The argument continued on the short drive home. Grace withdrew. When I saw that she had distanced herself from me I suddenly felt alone. I panicked. The rage had turned to fear and I insisted on closing the gap. I tried to hold her hand. She resisted, sat on the couch, and asked me to give her space. I sat right by her. I was consumed with anxiety, and the only way I thought I could handle it was to have Grace give in and allow me back into her world. She wanted no part of me. The only control I had was to follow her around and even lie beside her against her will. This went on late into the evening until both of us were exhausted. The next day I felt ashamed and apologized profusely. I am absolutely amazed that our dating lasted longer than a week as this would play out again and again. I truly don't know what possessed us to get married.

After returning from Las Vegas we picked up the two girls from their biological father's house, took them to an ice cream store, and showed them Grace's ring. They were completely floored. One of them cried; the other couldn't speak. Grace had been divorced from her third husband for less than a year. At the time I didn't get it. I could not get outside of myself long enough to understand how devastating it must have been for those two young girls. Our marriage was simply dropped on them like a ton of bricks. On the ride home I'm sure their prevailing thought was, *Here we go again.*

In June of 1990 we decided to move up to Seattle. I missed the northwest and SoCal was just too expensive. A previous business partner of mine said he had plenty of work for me, so we packed up a 27' moving van, left the girls to stay with family until we got settled, and began our trek north. We drove down the grapevine north of Los Angeles on I-5, and upon reaching the bottom stopped at a restaurant. I went to the restroom, and as I walked out I encountered a guy talking with Grace. He was telling her that our moving van had flames shooting out from the wheel wells. I guess I had been a little heavy on the brakes coming down the hill. But, instead of thanking the young man and running outside to inspect the damage, I confronted the Good Samaritan and asked why he was talking with Grace. My truck's brakes were on fire and my only concern was why he wasn't talking to me instead of my wife. My jealousy and lack of trust were out of control. And, it would get worse.

We rented a house owned by one of my previous clients in Edmonds, Washington. Edmonds is a cute, small town north of Seattle on the south end of Snohomish County and there we started to make a home and a family.. The only way I knew how to parent was what I was taught. That meant I was the king. Everything would revolve around me. If I wanted the heat turned up or the music turned down, I would have the final say. The only difference was that I would never lay a hand on the kids or Grace. I did my best to control in other ways.

Since my life was so completely different from how it was on the streets before prison, having a few alcoholic drinks did not seem like a big deal to me. Truth be told, one time while I was living with Dan and Helen, they were on vacation by themselves, and I got so drunk that I felt like I had the flu for a week. During the time Grace was in California to pick up the kids, I drank so much that I stumbled out of a Denny's lounge and still have no idea how I got home. Normally, when Grace and I went out to dinner I was comfortable with three drinks, but she was only comfortable if I had two. This, of course, would turn into an argument that would last until we were too tired to argue anymore.

Almost every day at lunch time, when I worked at my business partner's home in Ballard, I went to lunch at the same bar where I could flirt with the same bartender. And I always had a couple of beers. Just two. This was innocent enough to me. In my mind, I rarely got drunk. Just a couple times in four years. Well, maybe only six or seven times. Okay, ten at the most.

Within just a few months after moving to Edmonds I had to return to Ventura, California for bankruptcy court. Grace and I had wanted to start out our new life debt free, so we filed before our move. After court I planned to stay the night with my parents in Thousand Oaks and catch a flight home from LAX the next day. I was sitting on the couch with Mom and Dad in their chairs watching TV. Somehow the subject of my brother Dennis came up and Dad made a disparaging remark about him, indicating he was a worthless alcoholic just like our grandfather. Something in my soul just snapped. I would not have been able to react the same if it were about me. I was still convinced I got what I deserved. But something about the fact that Dennis was not there to defend himself set me off. And I got in touch with the cold and deliberate way in which my dad delivered the message. I saw my dad for the first time what he was. He was an asshole.

I stood up and told my parents I needed to run to the store. I walked out and shut the door behind me. It would be many years before I would speak with them again. Looking back, I see this was something I needed to do. I had been so consumed with gaining acceptance from them when what I really needed was for them to ask for forgiveness from me. But I didn't know that yet.

My dual life, selfishness, immaturity, jealousy, and rage continued. We went to church but were not actively involved. My faith had taken some big hits. I felt extremely uncomfortable around other Christians. The fact was I saw myself as better than they were. In addition, Grace would always find something wrong with the way she was being treated at church. We never sustained friendships with other couples. I believe my narcissism and immaturity drove many away.

When I was away from my house and family I did as I pleased and spent money I didn't have. Neither Grace nor I were responsible with finances. When I was paid, we took care of only those bills that would negatively impact our lives if left unpaid. We often sent only half the balance for phone or utilities. Many times one of us had to make the trip to a utility company with money to get the service turned back on. We moved around to a few houses or apartments and often paid late. When cell phones first hit the market I just had to have one "for business." I would often start an argument on the cellphone with Grace as I left work and continue for the next sixty minutes until I drove up to the front of my house. I was on the 60-minute per month plan, so those were extremely expensive arguments.

I also knew every porn and video store in Seattle. I never told anyone. There was some shame walking in, but incredible shame when walking out. Driving up Aurora Avenue at night I saw the prostitutes under street lights. I would slow down and their eyes would follow me. I watched in the rear view mirror as they waited to see if I would pull over and park. It gave me a sense of power. It was probably my only sense of power as my life with Grace simply sucked—for her and for me, and for the girls. In the words of a future therapist and friend, my life was "crazy making." Every day held drama. It was usually caused by me. Anything that held a mirror up to the mounting shame I felt deep within me was a catalyst for a blow up.

Let the Healing Begin

It was after one of those screaming matches that I refused to let Grace leave the room until my sense of abandonment was relieved. I recognized my apologies felt good for the moment, but I knew they would never be sustained, not without some help and not without some outside intervention.

In 1992 I found Crista—a ministry in Shoreline, Washington that loves God through serving people. They provided professional therapy services, both individual and group. I liked Gary Hamilton immediately as he did not have the stereotypical look of a therapist. Gary had been a Navy Seal and clearly conveyed the demeanor of someone who would not take any crap from anyone. I came to him needing to deal with my jealousy, and I honestly thought if I could just fix that my life would be roses.

Soon into our first session I shared with Gary that I had been in boys' homes and juvenile detention centers, and had spent five years in prison. I was quick to share that I was responsible for my actions and none of it was my parents' fault. I was proud of this self-awareness and was certain that Gary was impressed with my acknowledgement. When he probed into my early years I spoke of my mom and dad's discipline and parenting nonchalantly, almost as though I was describing mowing a lawn. At this point I began to wonder if I really needed any help. I sounded so healthy and there couldn't be anything new that this guy could drag out of me.

I don't know how Gary did it, but he took me back. Not as an adult, but as a child, facing my father—facing his wrath, reliving the fear. I heard the table saw in the basement. I saw him standing there, tapping his leg with the board. At first I couldn't talk as my throat felt like it was constricted. Eventually I cried and cowered. This was what I had been running from since I was five years old. Every drug I took, every drop I drank, every scream I uttered, and every pornographic image I took in—I used them all to stuff the same feelings in the past that I was now experiencing on the couch of Gary's office. I had never felt so exposed, so vulnerable. I was being operated on, sliced open with my guts ripped out, all without any anesthctic. This child was completely overcome by fear.

Suddenly, with Gary's guidance, I saw another man nearby. I don't know what Jesus actually looked like, but I knew it was him. He just looked at me then reached out his hand, but I was too scared; I didn't trust it. But he never wavered and never forced himself on me. His outstretched hand remained steady. His eyes softened me. His look took me in. Eventually I reached out and took his hand and I sobbed like never before. All the fear was gone. For the moment, at least.

This was my first real encounter with true healing. I recognized that trips to the altar did not induce magical potions that made the deep anger and rage go away. Healing would be hard earned. I had to do the work. It is sad to me that many religious groups still claim a prayer or a scripture will bring about healing. Prayer is good. Scripture is great. But it's not work.

Not long after my first meeting with Gary he asked that I write a letter to my father telling him how I felt about my early years growing up under his brutal discipline. I was working in South Seattle near a restaurant bar called Katell's. I was supposed to have this written for my next session with Gary, and I put it off until the last possible minute. Before my appointment, I went to Katell's and sat in a booth with a cup of coffee, my notepad, and pen. After about twenty minutes staring at a blank page I thought I might loosen up with a drink. I asked for a vodka and grapefruit juice—a double, since I would have only one. It worked and I began to write.

With one drink opening the dam I thought, *Why not another?* Now my pen was flying across the page, although the writing was growing more and more illegible. I had another double. I was being really productive but completely forgot about my appointment.

At some point I went to the bar to be closer to the source of the alcohol and switched to Wild Turkey. Luckily I called Stuart, my business partner before I got into my car. When Stuart arrived, I was completely smashed and walking around the bar and restaurant yelling, "Fuck my dad! Fuck my dad!" When taking me to his place, Stuart had to stop a few times to allow me to vomit. I said a number of times that I couldn't see. Later, Stuart told me he finally realized what it meant to be blind drunk.

The next week I went to my therapy session with Gary. He just smiled as he took my money for the missed appointment. He told me that writing the letter was obviously beneficial, only next time I might try it without medicating myself.

I also went to his group one day a week. The group members were all specifically chosen to resemble a typical dysfunctional family. I was the controller (although I had both controlling and co-dependent tendencies). Gary let me position myself early on as the caring helper. As I pontificated about how I used to be jealous and controlling but now understanding and nurturing, the co-dependent women in the group smiled at me and nodded. They expressed how they wished their spouse or boyfriend could be like me. Gary just sat back and let this happen. He had a plan.

One of the guys in the group was an openly gay man in his mid-twenties. He was extremely handsome, which was pointed out by some of the ladies multiple times. I had judged him early—not for being gay but for not standing up for himself. I thought he was a wuss. During one of our group sessions Gary looked me right in the eyes and asked, "You don't really like Shawn do you?"

Unable to lie or even consider my reputation, I told the truth. "No, I don't." I don't even remember the reasons I gave, but suddenly the dynamic shifted. I was no longer a favorite and was seriously disliked by most of the group members. While they previously seemed to struggle with standing up for themselves, they found their voices and I was on the receiving end of it. It also forced me to see who I had become and identified the long road it was going to take for me to truly change. The lie I had been selling to others I could no longer buy myself. I was exposed. And this was a good thing.

I continued to go to therapy, both group and individual, for a few years. I finally came to the point where the red hot ball of rage became more of an ember. I reached a milestone when I finally called my father and had a two-minute meaningful conversation with him. His voice had lost its power. My own inner child did not run trembling and I spoke to him as an adult without cussing or screaming. He eventually hung up on me, but I had maintained my composure. I felt strong. I felt alive. I felt powerful. It was a good moment.

I also came to the place where I recognized I did not own Grace, as simple and obvious as that sounds.

If she were to leave, I could not stop it. In fact, the desire to control everything around me continued to diminish over time. During this time, I met someone who pastored a small church in Everett who really understood Christian-based healing—the kind I had been experiencing at Crista Ministries. His name was Rich Swetman. We hit it off almost immediately. For the next couple of years we did church together, vacations and weekend nights, weekly golf, and individual and group therapy. Rich was able to explain the healing process and feelings around families of origin and toxic relationships in a way that I have not heard since. He introduced me to others in his circle, many of them pastors and ex-pastors. Although geographically separated, we remain friends to this day.

I do not believe I would have had any real success had it not been for those times in therapy when I allowed my inner-self to be exposed. But each moment of pain brought freedom and release of control. I'm extremely thankful to everyone who participated in this part of my recovery.

Donny Burke

In September of 1995, I was working with Jeff Jordan, owner of Fast Water Heater Company in Bellevue, Washington. I had developed dispatch and accounting software for Roto-Rooter and Day and Night Plumbing. Jeff was a young entrepreneur who believed in the benefits of leveraging software to drive the business and he contracted with me to purchase my software. We laugh now that the initial contract was for me to provide sixteen hours of customization. Ultimately I probably provided over 5,000 hours of services over the next ten years. Jeff ran his business on the first floor of his Bellevue home before moving it to a commercial property location. With his old space unused I moved in with our joint business, "DSoft" which specialized in developing dispatch and accounting software for service business. I believed then that I had the best product for the market, certainly from a dispatching perspective. Most of the other companies focused on accounting.

My life at that point was pretty good. Grace and I were no longer living in daily chaos. I made enough money to cover all of our expenses in addition to some extras. We were living in a townhome apartment in South Everett. I even went to AA meetings just down the street. I still did not understand the concept of AA, but I knew I shouldn't drink and I felt going to meetings helped.

One day I ran into Donny. He was living in an apartment close to Seattle Pacific University on Nickerson with his cat, Lucy. He was not the Donny I knew in prison. At forty years old he had become severely obese. He radiated insecurity, smoked pot daily, and desperately needed a job. I hired Donny at

$15 per hour, something I had no business doing. I'm not sure if it was due to curiosity or if I didn't want Donny to feel judged, but I decided to smoke pot with him. Other than the paranoia, I loved it.

A few days later I picked Donny up from the bus stop in Bellevue and we smoked a bowl. I have never been the kind of person who could wait until Friday night to partake recreationally. It became my medicine and I was addicted immediately. I would puff a few hits every hour or so throughout the day. I had started smoking cigarettes again as well. In my mind there was nothing wrong with pot. In fact, I convinced myself that I was more effective in my programming.

Grace was less than enthused, but seeing that she could do nothing about it, resigned herself to the fact that her once clean and sober husband was now a pothead. I'm convinced she stayed for financial reasons. She could not sustain her lifestyle on her own income.

Our business was thriving and I was bringing in $30,000 deals for hardware, software, and networking. I was excellent at selling and installing, but poor at support. In fact, I had no support plan and Donny didn't understand my software well enough to assist. There were times I simply did not answer the phone as I was not equipped in any way to handle a pissed off customer. Instead, we just stepped outside and smoked another bowl.

Around the middle of December I learned that Donny had an action against the state to receive disability. He claimed to be unable to live in general society due to all of his time in prison and institutions, going back to when he was fifteen. At his hearing about a week before Christmas in 1995, Donny had to describe to the judge how he got to the court house. On that day he had to walk since he was unable to take the bus due to anxiety. It was not an act. It was his real, daily existence. In order to receive disability assistance, he was forced to reveal how utterly pathetic his life had become. Even though the judge ruled in his favor, Donny never recovered from the humiliation. Sometimes "the truth will set you free" does not apply.

A week later on Christmas Day I called Donny but no one answered. I called his answering machine and used "Lucy" as the password. It worked. There had been a message from his previous girlfriend the evening before and then mine. Both unheard. I had a gut feeling and called the hospital in Everett. Donny had been admitted the night before but they could not release any information. I talked them into calling Donny's sister and asked that she call me right away with any information she could get.

Donny died of a heroin overdose. He had taken his own life. He had barely made it out the front door of the dope house and collapsed on the sidewalk. The junkies stripped him of his watch and money. In fact, they took his shirt and pants and left him naked on the concrete. Then someone called 9-1-1 and they all scattered like cockroaches with the light turned on.

My oldest stepdaughter, Shannon, held me as I cried, and other than the moments I took to inhale some marijuana I continued to cry for what must have been a month. I had to pull my car to the side of the rode many times as I simply could not see through my tears. I think I felt all of Donny's pain. There were times when I thought I was incapable of socializing, even to purchase something from the store, but I didn't have the balls to admit it. My body became run down and I got sick enough to go to my doctor. I had pneumonia and bronchitis. In addition, my doctor asked me if I had grandiose ideas and racing thoughts. This was an odd question. I told him I experienced something like that when I was deep into coding software. I did not tell him I was getting high every day.

Over the next few months I spent nearly all of my time in my office at Jeff's house. When Grace complained I told her it took all of my efforts to make DSoft successful. It was a source of contention between us, but again I did what I wanted and convinced myself that it was purely out of dedication. However, most of my time at work was spent looking at pornography, conversing in chat rooms, and, of course, getting high. By now I had sales in Alaska, Portland, Seattle, Boise, and Spokane, but the most recent sales were unsuccessful due to lack of support and they wanted their money back. I felt safe in my office. I just turned off the phone and smoked another bowl.

One Saturday morning I woke up in a hotel room. I wasn't sure where I was and had to look at the guest book to see the name of the hotel. I was at the Crown Plaza in Redondo Beach, California. To the best of my memory at the time, I was there to start up a new business, but I had no idea what or why. I had some pot but didn't know if I purchased it there or brought it on the plane. I spent some time on the beach and returned home to Everett.

I went back to my doctor and confessed that I had been smoking pot. When I told him about my journey to Redondo Beach he asked me again about whether I had racing thoughts and grandiose ideas. I thought about it. It was entirely possible. My doctor diagnosed me as being Bipolar or Manic Depressive and prescribed Lithium. I couldn't argue with him. It made sense. But after just a couple of weeks I quit taking it. It slowed my mind down too much and I was unable to write code.

That started me on a downward spiral that ended July 19, 1996. During the late spring and summer months I left Grace and went on a manic binge that included purchasing $10,000 worth of music equipment using my company credit card (guaranteed by Jeff). I traveled to Anacortes, Washington, Kalispell, Montana, and Eugene, Oregon. I was on the run again. I smoked pot and drank. If I ran out of money I snuck back to my office and took something that I could sell. Eventually there was nothing left. I went to downtown

Seattle and managed to hustle free drinks at a gay bar. I drank enough to convince myself I should wait in a back alley for someone to walk by so I could rob them. No one came. I drove drunk to the University district, parked my truck on the avenue, and went looking for something to get me high. I purchased enough crystal meth to kill a horse from a street dealer, and he gave me a used needle. I just didn't care. I went back to my truck, prepared the powder in a bottle cap, took off my tennis shoes, and tried tying off my arm with the shoe laces. I was too drunk and neglected to remove the laces; I needed help. Just then a man walked by. I flagged him down and asked him if he would help tie off my arm so I could run this meth up my veins.

This man started to talk to me in a soothing voice. He asked, "Do you really want to do that? Are you sure?" I looked at him. He was a healthy specimen, very handsome with long golden hair. He continued to talk to me in that smooth voice. He reached out and I handed him the meth and the needle. I looked away for just a second and looked back. He was gone. He had just vanished. I put my shoes on and walked to a nearby bar, lifted the pay phone off the hook, and dialed my stepdaughter Lisa's phone number. She let me be the crying drunk, blubbering about how I missed my life, about how I'd screwed it up again. She told me she loved me. I cried some more. I asked if I could spend the night at Tom's (her brother) house. Tom said yes. I got into my truck and drove the twenty or so miles doing the one-eye on the freeway trying desperately not to hit anyone. Maybe the angel who talked me out of killing myself was steering my truck too.

The next day I flew to Southern California to a treatment center. The CFO was Grace's brother, so it was a free bed. I was absolutely determined that this would not be a wasted opportunity. And, it wasn't. I entered the treatment center nearly nineteen years ago and have not used drugs or alcohol since.

Probably the most powerful intervention I would receive came from a woman counselor just a week after I arrived. By now I was feeling physically better, although still scared from my manic binge. They immediately put me back on Lithium. In group time I still thought I was smarter and better than everyone else. I was often asked to sit on the floor to humble myself. I had no problem with that and sat there, proudly demonstrating how well I took instruction.

This female counselor asked me one day to write an angry letter to my mother. Really? To my mother? She was just the sweetest person in the world; ask anyone! But I said okay, I would do that. The next day in our session she asked me to show her what I'd written. I began to explain some incredible insight I'd had and went on and on about it. Suddenly this petite woman stood up, slammed her hand down on the table, leaned into me, and asked, "Why don't you do as you're fucking told!?"

I bristled at first. She can't talk to me like that! But she never wavered and kept her authoritative position. We stared at each other and it finally hit me. She was right. I always thought I had the answer. Really, no one has ever been able to tell me anything unless I agreed with it. She told me, "Just because you have a thought, it doesn't mean it is right." I have to wonder where I'd be if this awesome counselor had not said the right thing at the right time. My chances of relapsing were high. I was told by the treatment staff that I had more reasons to use again than I did to stay sober. I was convinced I was an alcoholic. To clarify, I have an allergy to alcohol. If someone were allergic to strawberries, the manifestation of that allergy might be a rash. Having an allergy to alcohol means if I were to consume it, the manifestation of the allergy is not a rash, but an uncontrollable craving for more. In addition, I will always have an inclination to deaden my pain. This means if I drink I'm doomed. I can never control it. Ever.

I'm also convinced that my recovery required multiple points of attack. AA without therapy would not have provided the healing I experienced so many times in Gary's and Rich's offices. But therapy alone did not give me the understanding that I was an alcoholic and an addict. I believe God was with me at every moment and ultimately He gets the credit for any success I have or will have, but I had to be willing to let him help me.

I was thirty-six when I began to finally experience

a little maturity. It took an incredible amount of failure to reach that point in my life. It took every ounce of my will to feel the pain I ran from for so long. I don't know what was worse, the dramatic life I lead on the streets or experiencing rage sparked by jealousy and feelings of abandonment. Was it the fear I had walking the back steps to the hospital in prison wondering who might jump out and stab me, or the fear I had when Grace walked out of the room, afraid she would not come back?

I returned to Seattle after six weeks of treatment and made amends to Jeff. I'm forever grateful to him that he allowed me back into his world after the decisions I made which cost him personally. I continued to work for him for many years and we remain friends to this day.

Grace and I got back together but separated after two years and eventually divorced. It's funny how little we had in common after the crazy making life had left us. I remain close to her son, Tom, and daughters Shannon and Lisa.

In 2008 I came upon on opportunity to assist Microsoft with developing their ERP solution, Dynamics AX. This positioned me well to lead the technical side of large enterprise implementations. With the continued uptake of this software in the United States, I see a clear path to continue this line of work until I retire.

Finally, I married my current wife, Kathy Forbes, in August of 2000. She has never seen me take a drink of alcohol nor take any drugs—not because I hide it, but because I have not indulged since that night in 1996 in the University District in Seattle. I also had the joy of raising her son Kevin from the age of nine. Kathy has been and is the love of my life and we are looking forward to growing old together.

I started writing this book while traveling to client sites last year. Ever since I visited MacLaren School for Boys in 2006 I recognized I had something that most people do not have. The fact that I was at one time a youth inmate at MacLaren and now earn a significant living as an IT professional literally buys me 30 to 45 minutes of time with at-risk youth where they actually listen and want to hear what I have to say. None of them want to be there. And they all want to know how to get out of that fast, reckless life. I feel I have an obligation and a responsibility to share my pain, my joy of redemption, and process of recovery. I could never make amends to every person I injured on my journey. But maybe I can say I'm sorry by passing along my story to those who feel they have no hope.

The day I stopped drinking and using is the day I began to grow up. It could not, would not, have happened otherwise. The fact is I had a tough start. Was it fair? No. But the old saying, "Tell it to the judge" rings true. Regardless of how I grew up I was still responsible for everything I did. Maturity taught me that I was not responsible for what others did, namely my parents. No one deserves to be hit or devalued. But it cannot be an excuse. Trust me, I know—the judge really doesn't want to hear it. Spiritual, mental, and emotional maturity is possible despite what has been done to us and what we have done to others.

On July 25, 2014, my mother passed away at eighty-six years old after being scalded by hot water in the shower. I believe my mother always carried some guilt for standing by during our abuse. If she could do it all over again I am convinced she would have made different decisions.

On March 5, 2015 my father passed away as well. He and mom were married fifty-eight years and he simply did not want to live another day without her. I can't say my father and I had a good relationship in his later years, but we did reconcile prior to his passing. Over the fifteen years prior to his death, my father apologized for his abuse and said more than once that he wished he could go back in time and turn the board on himself. I feel honored that I received an apology. Many abuse victims do not.

Larry and Pam Poggemeyer and I have remained friends to this day. In fact, during the time that both my mother and father were in the hospital in their last days, Kathy and I stay with them. We never get tired of telling the story of the young adults returning to ask me to stay over the weekend. I am forever thankful to them for taking Dennis and me in.

Dennis died in an auto accident November 6, 2000 in Missoula, Montana, and I am grateful he finally found peace. I'm also grateful that my parents passed prior to the release of this book. I had to tell the truth and I was concerned about how they would be affected. However, had they been alive today and able to read it, I would not have changed a single word.

In closing, I'd like to say to the sixty-year-old who has screwed up more times than he/she can remember: it might just take a feisty little counselor standing on a box, looking you in the eye and telling you you're full of shit. And maybe that person is right. To the sixteen-year-old who is already floating down the rapids of the juvenile system: put everything you have into finding something that gives you value. Maybe it's singing. Maybe it's programming websites. Maybe it's serving at the local homeless shelter. I'm sorry that someone in your life said or did things to you that seriously undercut your sense of personal worth. But you can stop the madness now. You're worth it.

EPILOGUE

I parked my Ford Explorer in the Kmart parking lot in South Salem just where Highway-22 ended and the city began. After briefly stretching my legs and taking a long gulp of water, I began to head south on my Trek mountain bike, passing the airport on my right and the four-lane highway on my left. Within twenty minutes I rode by the Oregon Corrections Center where my father told me I would end up. Twenty-five years prior I sat in the back of a smoky car riding home from church on the same road, my only concern was wondering if we would stop to eat or go straight home. Now I concentrated on establishing a good rhythm while giving the speeding cars on my left enough room as the low fog had not yet lifted.

Twelve miles later I entered the town of Stayton and thought about stopping for a cup of coffee, but my legs would not stop churning. I took another gulp of water while riding past Stayton Grade School where I received the first five years of my education. I was flooded with memories: trying to fit in, trying to make friends, all while keeping secrets. I rode on.

While Rollercoaster Hill was the longest and steepest grade on Cole School Road, it was by no means the only hill I had to conquer on this quest. Turning off Stayton-Scio Road onto Cole School Road, I had to lift off the bike seat as my legs began to complain at the immediate incline. A steep but quick slope, my quads gained temporary reprieve at the top.

I passed the Mertz's who provided the strawberry fields every year for income. Before I reached Sandner Road I was challenged by the second longest and steepest hill. My legs were screaming on the way up, riding in first gear with each pedal rotation gaining no more than one or two feet of distance. But I would win this challenge as well and the road finally began to level out.

Five minutes later I was parallel with the house where I grew up at the top of Rollercoaster Hill. I saw the telephone on the other side of the road that I threw rocks at while waiting for the school bus. The property was now fenced in and the big oak tree in the front yard was missing. The front of the house was facing south and was no longer painted white. But none of these changes were as dramatic as the changes that occurred inside of me. I will never forget the things that happened in the upstairs bedroom, but they no longer crippled my ability to live an abundant life.

I pedaled on and began the descent on Rollercoaster Hill. I popped my Trek into 21st gear and my legs were quickly spinning faster than the resistance. I was only a third of the way back up this monster hill before I downshifted into first gear as my legs began to burn. Another ten feet and my body and my mind wanted to quit. No one would fault me for stopping and walking the rest of the way as I'd always done before. I could end the agony instantly. I thought about all the times in my life when I quit. So often I took the easier road. Everyone would understand if I just stopped the pain. But not today.

My heart, and maybe even my inner child, would simply not let me stop. Another ten feet, and another. I was halfway up. I simply refused to stop. I could not stop. My legs felt as though they were on fire. They were weakening. Another ten feet. And ten more.

Finally, as my right leg pushed for what felt like the millionth time that day, the resistance lessened. The same with my left leg. And my right again and my left and . . . the road leveled out. I reached the top. My feet touched the ground for the first time since I left the Kmart parking lot in Salem, about twenty miles before. I had finally conquered Rollercoaster Hill. As an adult, the hill was as ominous that day as when I was six years old. It was the same, but I was not. I had a quiet moment as I turned and looked at the challenge I had just overcome. There was no fanfare. There was no applause from the gallery. It was just me and my own sense of accomplishment. I won.

I took another long drink of water, turned my bike around, and began my descent, shifting my Trek into 21st gear gaining as much speed as I could for the hill on the other side.

About the Author

Dwaine Casmey survived the streets by doing the things street people do – hustling, stealing, robbing, drugs, among other degrading acts in order to live for just one more day. He spent the better part of ten years incarcerated in boys' homes, shelter homes, juvenile detention, and adult prisons. Because he missed out on developing a personal sense of value early in life, he treated himself and others with no respect. He was destined to be just another statistic: a repeat offender who would eventually end up permanently incarcerated or as another body in a morgue.

Today Dwaine is a Managing Consultant for a global information technology company and manages technical delivery for multi-million dollar enterprise software projects. With twenty-six years of software design experience and over two years assisting Microsoft with developing its global enterprise business application, Dwaine is recognized as a technical thought leader in the ERP (Enterprise Resource Planning) industry.

As a result of his transformation, Dwaine began to feel a burning desire to share the story of his journey out of the muck and the mire into a life of love and freedom in order to provide hope for those who are lost, including their families watching from the grandstands. He wants anyone and everyone with a sense of diminished value to believe that change and high value can be attained, regardless of their circumstances, and it is his hope that his story will inspire change and bring hope to the lost. Dwaine lives in Castle Rock, CO with his wife Kathy.

Appendix A

DEPARTMENT OF HUMAN RESOURCES
CHILDREN'S SERVICES DIVISION
POLK BRANCH

326 MAIN   •   P.O. BOX 198   •   DALLAS, OREGON   •   97338

June 30, 1976

                    COURT REPORT

RE: Casmey, Dwaine

Purpose of the Hearing

The purpose of the hearing is to adjudicate three petitions;
one for theft in the second degree comitted on June 8, 1976,
one for possession of liquor by a minor comitted on the sixth
day of June, 1976, and one for criminal mischief in the
second degree comitted May 1, 1976. I also am ready to pro-
ceed with the disposition phase of the hearing once the ad-
judication is out of the way.

Background Information

Dwaine Casmey was brought into our office on April 27, 1976,
with the request that he be placed in foster care. They re-
quested this because they indicated that they did not seem
to be able to control him, that he had in the past been
sneaking out at night, that he had come home on several occasions drunk and also just recently he had become involved
in the theft of some money from a woman's purse. I attempted
to talk with the Casmeys about having Dwaine remain in the
home while we worked with him on trying to solve the problem.
They, however, were adamant in wanting him placed in foster
care. Dwaine at this time, also, was refusing to return home.
Because of this, I reluctantly placed Dwaine in shelter care.
I originally had hoped that maybe by working with the parents
we would be able to return Dwaine to the home sometime after
he had had time to cool down a little bit and the parents had
had time to cool down a little bit. This, however, has not
worked out, the parents have remained adamant that they do
not want him to return home and Dwaine has also continued to
refuse to return home. Also, I have talked to ████████████,
who has been counseling with Dwaine and she feels that it
would not be in his best interests to return home at this time.
She indicated that she felt Mr. Casmey partioularly was a
very rigid person who was unwilling to compromise in anyway in
dealing with his son, Dwaine. She felt that Dwaine was under
a lot of pressure because of this and that he was very emotionally upset and in need of some intensive counseling.

247

Since Dwaine has been in shelter care, he has been involved in
several incidents which have resulted in his being placed in
detention. In the early part of May, he lost his temper at the
shelter home and put his fist through one of the windows. A week
or so after that, he ran away with one of the girls from the
shelter home. He subsequently was transferred to the shelter home
in Salem. On June 6, he returned to the shelter home in an
intoxicated state and two days later on June 8, he was involved
in shoplifting a carton of cigarettes. Since the June 8, incident
Dwaine has been in detention.

Originally after we decided that Dwaine would not be able to return home, I attempted to locate a foster home for Dwaine, however,
with his many behavior problems; I have come to the conclusion that
a foster home would not be able to deal with him and he needs to
be placed in a youth care center. I made contact with several center
including Youth Adventures, Youth for Christ and ███████ Manor.
The first two did not have any openings, however, ███████ Manor
does have an opening and they have indicated they will take Dwaine
on a weeks trial basis. At the end of the week, they will then
decide whether they think they can help him and if so they will
accept him into their program.

Recommendation

My recommendation is that Dwaine be made a ward of the court with
care, custody and supervision granted to CSD. Our plan is to
place him at Hawthorne Manor. We will not know for sure until his
first week's trial visit is completed whether he will be staying
there, but if not I will plan on bringing the matter back into
court to modify disposition.

Respectfully submitted,

████████████

Caseworker

RMM:dw

Appendix B

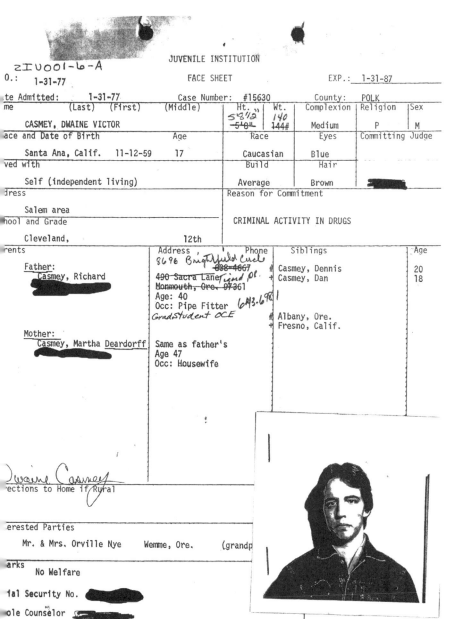

ZIU001-6-A

O.: 1-31-77   FACE SHEET   EXP.: 1-31-87

te Admitted: 1-31-77			Case Number: #15630		County: POLK		
me (Last) (First)		(Middle)	Ht. 5'8½" ~~5'8"~~	Wt. 140 144#	Complexion Medium	Religion P	Sex M
CASMEY, DWAINE VICTOR							
ace and Date of Birth		Age	Race	Eyes	Committing Judge		
Santa Ana, Calif. 11-12-59		17	Caucasian	Blue			
ved with			Build	Hair			
Self (independent living)			Average	Brown	▆▆▆▆▆		
dress			Reason for Commitment				
Salem area			CRIMINAL ACTIVITY IN DRUGS				
hool and Grade							
Cleveland,		12th					

rents	Address 8696 Brightfield Circle	Phone ~~838-4607~~	Siblings	Age
Father: Casmey, Richard	~~490 Sacra Lane~~ Tigard Ol. ~~Monmouth, Ore. 07361~~ Age: 40 Occ: Pipe Fitter 643-698 / Grad Student OCE	# +	Casmey, Dennis Casmey, Dan Albany, Ore. Fresno, Calif.	20 18
Mother: Casmey, Martha Deardorff	Same as father's Age 47 Occ: Housewife			

Dwaine Casmey

ections to Home if Rural

erested Parties

Mr. & Mrs. Orville Nye   Wemme, Ore.   (grandp

arks   No Welfare

ial Security No. ▆▆▆▆

ole Counselor ▆▆▆▆

Appendix C

PSYCHIATRIC REPORT

DWAINE CASMEY   #15630   February 24, 1977

This is a 17 year old boy who was referred for a psychiatric examination with the following statement: "Heavy drug and alcohol usage, a very bright personable young man who seems to be destroying himself. Program and counseling approach suggestions". The report as provided by the Polk County Juvenile Court was reviewed. The various significant details particularly in regard to his failure in adjusting to community placements will not be repeated here.

In this examination Dwaine was quite verbal, showed appropriate affect, had some intellectual insight into his difficulties. He did not exhibit any evasiveness and was able to describe his feelings in good details. He gave a history of extreme passivity both in the home and in his social life, described himself as a "tag along" who was simply unable to express himself well. He gave examples of his father ordering him around at home and his inability to ask "why". Apparently, he had a better relationship with his mother. He described himself as coming from a good Christian home and playing an organ in the church for five years. Just about the time when he entered active adolescence, he began to "hate himself" primarily because of his passivity and not being able to take a stand on any issue with peer group and simply going along. He added "I did not know who I was". He would feel resentful and depressed underneath but at the same time, was unable to share his feelings with his parents. He did not have any close friends, and therefore, that door was shut to him. He carried this burden of being inadequate, passive, and "being worthless" for some time before he entered the drug scene. Apparently, Dwaine has used Marijuana, Barbituates, and Cocaine and also indulged in excessive alcohol. He added "when I would take dope I would feel different about myself and I liked it". Obviously, his self-image became damaged to the point that he became anxious, depressed, guilt ridden, and turned to drugs and alcohol. He also described himself as very adaptive. He explained this by saying that he was generally easy to get along with, likeable, and he wondered whether he was a "master con artist". He did not like to go along with the system or to manipulate people but he did not have any confidence in himself to even have any perception whether he was being right or wrong. He was generally in good contact with reality and there was no evidence of any psychosis or mental disorder. I spent some time in counseling with this boy primarily exphasizing his understanding and his behavior and learning alternative ways of coping with anxiety and depression. It should be stated here that three or four months back he put burning cigarettes on his left forearm though he did not think that it was "self-punishment". Generally, we have a very bright but passive and inadequate young man who has never learned to express his feelings, share with others or perhaps trust other people. He has over the years lost his self-confidence and has had a very poor self-image. He is in need of intensive counseling. I suggest the following: 1) Counselor be designated for him who could see this boy twice a week on a regular basis and have a conference with me every month for a few minutes regarding the outcome of the counseling sessions. 2) Family counseling with the boy and his parents might be quite helpful as we need their support in helping this youngster express himself and find his worthwhileness. He is not in need of any medication regime at this time.

PKP:cw

Consulting Psychiatrist

Appendix D

INITIAL HOME AND COMMUNITY: CASMEY, DWAINE VICTOR   1/31/77   1/31/87
Polk County - █████████   DOB: 11/12/59   #15630

Parents: Richard and Martha Casmey 490 Sacre Lane Monmouth, OR 97361 838-4667.

I. HOME

The home is located in the Northeast part of Monmouth at 490 Sacre Lane. The home is a relatively new home, ranch style, purchaed one year ago by the parents of Dwaine Casmey. It is a three bedroom home, very neatly furnished clean and well-arranged.

Mrs. Casmey is a housewife; her husband is a student at OCE working toward a Master's Degree in counseling. The parents are not able to describe any particular problems in their relationship with the boy; they are unable to detect or make an observation about why the boy has been an acting out boy or why he has turned to the use of drugs. In discussing the relationship with Dwaine it is observed that they do not admit or acknowledge difficulties with him; they indicate that he is well behaved in the home but he is not able to appropriately behave himself when he is out in the community. The parents do say that the boy is extremely good at manipulating; is very intelligent and never sees any accomplishment as being worthwhile. They say he is able to do extremely well academically; he is very musically inclined and is able to succeed in anything that he makes an attempt at, but does not recognize this as being important.

Parents suggest that the boy is in good physical condition; he is healthy a rather small built person, but is in good health at this time.

II. COMMUNITY

Court:

5/3/76 Crim. Mischief II   Petition filed but no disposition indicated.
5/18/76 Runaway   Petition filed and dismissed.
6/6/76 Minor in Possession   "   " - no action taken
6/9/76 Theft II   "   "   dismissed
9/17/76 Crim. Act. in Drugs "   "   boy placed on suspended comm. to MacLaren.
12/6/76 Running away from ██████ Program   Petition filed on 1/25/77 again charged with runaway; however the records not clear as to where that runaway occurred from. The boy was committed to MacLaren on 1/31/77.

The police: No comments from local police. The family has lived in the Monmouth area since June, 1973.

School: The boy last attended Central High School at Independence, no other informatic relating to school, except that the boy is intelligent and can achieve very well academically. The parents suggest that the boy started using drugs at Central High Scl

III. RECOMMENDATION

Counseling approach: Dwaine needs to improve the image that he has of himself. If the observation is accurate from the parents, it appears that the boy is able to accomplish, but has not as yet accomplished anything that he sees as being worthwhile.

School: This should be either GED or regular high school whichever program the boy gets involved in, he must be chanllenged, otherwise he becomes bored and will not continue in whatever program it may be.

253

INITIAL HOME AND COMMUNITY: CASMEY, DWAINE V.

Parents indicate that the boy has not had work experience to any extent
accept for restaurant work in the Salem area. The parents add that the boy
is a gifted musician however, has not been involved in playing professionally
except for the family church.

Home visit resource: Parents.

Resource involvement: Parents will visit boy regularly. Mr. Casmey is a
practicum student in Juvenile Parole and will be seeing the boy on occassion
at MacLaren School.

Tentative placement plan: Parole to parents, if the boy concurs with this
sort of planning.

March 1, 1977

Appendix E

Department of Human Resources
CHILDREN'S SERVICES DIVISION
MacLaren School
ROUTE 1, BOX 37, WOODBURN, OREGON 97071 PHONE 981-9531

ROBERT W. STRAUB
GOVERNOR

Address all correspondence
to the Superintendent

December 16, 1977

Honorable [redacted]
Judge of the Circuit Court
Polk County Courthouse
Dallas, Oregon 97338

Attention: [redacted] Director
Polk County Juvenile Department

Dear [redacted]:

RE: Dwaine Victor Casmey DOB: 11-12-59

We are writing to request the release of Dwaine Victor Casmey who was committed to the Children's Services Division by action of your court on April 22, 1976.

Dwaine Victor Casmey was admitted to MacLaren School by order of your court on January 31, 1977 for "Criminal Activity in Drugs".

Since Dwaine's commitment to the Children's Services Division he has exhausted all programs pertinent to his rehabilitative interests. Dwaine is currently assigned to our security cottage, Detention II, and is satisfactorily meeting all program criteria expected of him. This student has successfully completed all of his high school credits for graduation. Dwaine has also exhibited stable behavior patterns and has expressed concern for his post-MacLaren living patterns. His rapport with his peers and cottage staff has been satisfactory, with a degree of increased openness. Due to Dwaine's suitable performance in the Detention II program, it has not been necessary for him to undergo extensive psychological counseling.

Dwaine became eighteen on November 12, 1977. His post-release plans consist of his parents providing temporary housing for Dwaine prior to independent living. He plans on doing apprentice work for his father, who is a regional supervisor for the International Pipefitter's Union.

Based on the above, we are respectfully requesting that Dwaine Victor Casmey's commitment to the Children's Services Division of Oregon be

Casmey, Dwain Victor
December 16, 1977
Page 2

terminated and his wardship vacated.

Sincerely,

General Superintendent
Juvenile Corrections Services

Resident Superintendent

BKH/BA/se